# Race for a Change
# in Continuing and
# Higher Education

THE CUTTING EDGE

*Series Editors*:
*Susan Weil*, Head of Higher Education Development and Fellow in Organizational Learning at the Office for Public Management, and Visiting Lecturer for the Centre for Higher Education Studies, University of London.
*Malcolm Tight*, Senior Lecturer in Continuing Education, University of Warwick.

This series deals with critical issues and significant developments in continuing education, focusing on its impact on higher education.

*Current titles in the series*:

Tom Bourner *et al.*: *Part-time Students and their Experience of Higher Education*
Chris Duke: *The Learning University*
Mal Leicester: *Race for a Change in Continuing and Higher Education*
David Smith and Michael Saunders: *Other Routes: Part-time Higher Education Policy*

# Race for a Change
in Continuing and
Higher Education

MAL LEICESTER

The Society for Research into Higher Education
& Open University Press

Open University Press
Celtic Court
22 Ballmoor
Buckingham
MK18 1XW

and

1900 Frost Road, Suite 101
Bristol, PA 19007, USA

First Published 1993

A catalogue record of this book is available from the British Library

ISBN 0 335 09767 7 (pb)   0 335 09768 5 (hb)

Library of Congress catalog number available

Typeset by Graphicraft Typesetters Ltd, Hong Kong
Printed in Great Britain by St Edmundsbury Press Ltd,
Bury St Edmunds, Suffolk

*To Hilda Leicester and Jane Phillips-Bell*
*with love and thanks*

# Contents

Series Editor's Preface                                                    viii
Acknowledgements                                                             x

Introduction                                                                 1

**Part 1   Antiracist Continuing Education: Agent and Model**               7
 1   Continuing Education as Change Agent: Inreach and
     Outreach                                                                9
 2   Conceptual Clarification: 'Racism' and 'Antiracist
     Education'                                                             16
 3   Conceptual Clarification. 'Antiracist Continuing Education'            23
 4   Practising What We Preach: Departmental Change                         29
 5   Change Agents and Models: A UCACE Survey Revisited                     40

**Part 2   Continuing Antiracist Education: The University
           Transformed**                                                   47
 6   Coming of Age: The Mature University                                   49
 7   Outreach: Antiracist Access                                           59
 8   Access and Maintaining Academic Standards                             66
 9   Inreach: Accessibility and the Antiracist University                  77
10   Higher Education for All                                              95

     *Appendix 1   Resources to Support Antiracist Work in Post-16
        Education*                                                         108
     *Appendix 2   UCACE Recommendations*                                  119
     *Appendix 3   Antiracist Higher Education Questionnaire*              121
     *Notes*                                                               127
     *Bibliography*                                                        131
     *Index*                                                               136
     *The Society for Research into Higher Education*                      143

# Series Editor's Preface

*The Cutting Edge* series is based on the premise that social, demographic, economic, political and technological trends are now combining to ensure that virtually all institutions of higher education are concerned to open their provision to new kinds of students. It takes issues that are being illuminated at the margins and demonstrates their relevance to mainstream higher education provision.

Students from different cultural and ethnic backgrounds – not just from overseas, but within Britain and the rest of Europe – are amongst the many in the wider population who are willing and able to benefit from higher education. They have all too often been denied access hitherto.

In *Race for a Change*, the author begins with the experience of continuing education departments in relation to 'race' and culture. Their efforts to widen opportunity to black and ethnic minority students provide the starting point for her arguments for change. She suggests that the shift from an elitist to a mass higher education system, and investment in new forms of 'outreach' (i.e. credit-based structures, progression routes, accreditation of prior learning) are not sufficient to achieve the changes from which black and ethnic minority students and indeed all students would benefit. In particular, she calls for the establishment of an antiracist higher education system.

In keeping with the intention of the series, she argues that an emphasis on antiracism would do greater justice to what she sees as the core purposes of higher education: the pursuit and dissemination of disciplined and worthwhile knowledge and understanding. She speaks of achieving an 'ethically and epistemologically desirable transformation of higher education' that would benefit all: black and white colleagues, women and men with a diversity of experience, cultural background and perspective.

She believes that CE departments have a vital role to play as role models and agents of change in such an endeavour. She suggests that the attention paid to outreach must be balanced with equal attention to 'inreach'. In other words, mainstream thinking and practice require a more fundamental transformation. Only in this way can it support new kinds of students and new forms of educational gain relevant to needs for continuous learning in a diverse and rapidly changing society.

The author is herself a white woman who continues to struggle with such issues across the range of education provision. She makes clear the stance from which she writes, demonstrating her commitment to continuous improvement and challenge focused on the system itself. Breinburg (1987) suggests that white professionals tend to focus upon access and under-representation whereas black professionals and students are more concerned with curricular content and presentation. But Leicester clearly shows herself to support a view of access concerned with 'collective and political issues of knowledge and power' rather than one that ignores 'cultural barriers which isolate and abstract the individual learner, and which tend to reduce the issue to one wholly resolvable in technical and institutional terms' (Parry 1989).

Many who are committed to wider access are struggling with the question of whether educational innovations of one kind – intended to benefit traditionally under-represented groups – can occur without disturbing taken-for-granted behaviours, attitudes, structures, processes and outcomes. Many are also concerned about the contradictions between what is claimed on behalf of higher education, and what is actually experienced in reality by different groups of students. Although much remains to be understood about such experience, I believe that the distinctive contribution of this book is that it begins to fill the vacuum of writing on such issues for higher education at a time of such rapid change. It is hoped that further contributions, providing opportunities to re-think what we may all too readily take for granted, will follow in its wake.

*Susan Weil*

# Acknowledgements

I wish to thank John Skelton for encouraging me to write this book and Susan Weil for guiding me towards a better final version. As will be apparent, Chris Duke has stimulated my thinking about continuing education, and colleagues in the UCACE working group on 'provision for minority ethnic groups' have influenced my claims about antiracism in that context. For more specific services, I must thank Lesley Leicester who typed the final manuscript so efficiently while simultaneously teaching me to use a wordprocessor.

Yet deeper gratitude is owed to Tessa Lovell, my excellent research assistant, who worked closely with me on the two surveys which inform Chapters 5 and 10, and Carolyn Sugden who produced the extremely useful post-16 resource list in Appendix 1.

Finally, warm thanks to Morag Macdonald McNeil for the loan of her comfortable home in Barra where, overlooking sea and sky, much of the writing was done.

# Introduction

It is intended that the series of which this book is a part address the critical issues at the cutting edge of university continuing education. I shall argue that 'race' and culture issues have just such transformative power as this intention implies. Indeed, my main thesis is that not only would an antiracist multicultural approach transform university continuing education, but that antiracist continuing education could itself prove a cutting edge for higher education *per se*.

The *Cutting Edge* metaphor is particularly apt in relation to antiracist multicultural education in at least three ways. An antiracist, pluralist approach will transform *adult* education in higher education and other contexts; adult and continuing education departments are potential change agents in higher education with regard to the development of antiracist higher education and in other ways; while 'race' and culture issues, properly understood, could empower higher education in its most central tasks.

My aim is to justify these claims through an exploration of the issues and their change potential, focusing on both theoretical and relatively more practical considerations and incorporating an analysis of relevant empirical research. I hope to stimulate thinking about theoretical aspects of antiracist continuing and higher education and to offer some guidance for practice both in terms of student learning and of securing relevant institutional change.

The 1985 Swann Report, *Education For All*, encouraged schools in their development of an antiracist multicultural education and, to date, the main focus of institutional and classroom development and of related writing and research has been the school rather than the post-school sector. This relative lack of post-school attention is reflected in the limited amount of good practice or attention to such concerns in universities.

It is my experience that the 'higher' one goes through the education sectors, the more one finds resistance to progressive antiracist and pluralist change. (This is not, of course, particularly surprising. The more privileged, elitist and hierarchical the arena, the more resistance to democratizing developments one might expect to find.)

There is a sense in which the book as a whole constitutes an answer to two dual questions: What would antiracist university adult education and higher education be like, and how can they be (relatively) achieved? The first question involves considerations of institutional structures, access, research, pedagogy, curriculum and clientele. The second question directs attention to staff development, institutional change and to departments of adult and continuing education as agents of change reaching across their own university to bring progressive developments into the mainstream of the institution, and also reaching outside to the communities it serves.

I explore the idea of departments of continuing education as change agents driving antiracist changes within their own university, and 'race' issues as a kind of barium meal in the institution, showing up the structures and practices by which universities perpetuate privilege and maintain entrenched power. I use the relatively new department of continuing education at Warwick, of which I am a member, as a case study.

Although antiracist education should be developed across the education system as a whole, and although many issues span the school and post-school divide, there is one significant difference: all children must go to school, whereas older students choose to continue their education. This means that post-school there are additional issues about recruitment, selection, competition for places, and about fees. Some black British groups are underrepresented in higher level courses in further education and in all courses in higher education (Taylor 1992). This issue of *inclusion and exclusion* is important in relation to racism. Who benefits most from post-school educational opportunities and how can universities become more accessible to minority ethnic groups? Access and outreach issues rightly have a high profile in continuing education – partly for pragmatic reasons and the economic need for more clients, and partly for ethical considerations about equity and equal opportunities, I shall argue that widening access to the universities will improve, not dilute, the quality of higher education.

Antiracist educational issues fall into two categories: issues of provision for minority ethnic groups, including this opening up of the university to 'non-traditional' students, and also the broader issues concerning the need, in a multicultural society, to develop a non-ethnocentric curriculum for all students. (Although my research projects to identify good practice in higher education were conducted in British universities, the principles inherent in the exemplifications chosen have a more general applicability.)

I take the major aim of higher education to be the pursuit and dissemination of disciplined and worthwhile knowledge and understanding. There are two main tasks in this – academics seek to add to our collective knowledge through research and they seek to facilitate the individual student's knowledge and understanding through teaching. I include an analysis of the epistemological underpinning of my claim that an antiracist and pluralist education would facilitate this double-tiered generation of knowledge and enrich academic achievements.

In addition to these epistemological considerations, I seek in general to justify my varied and interrelated claims through the argument and empirical data of which I make use. Justification comes to an end, however, and rests on a bedrock of those ultimate values by which we justify our judgements. These basic values, being ultimate and justificatory, cannot themselves be justified. At this level, the bedrock of this work and its vision of continuing and higher education, lie ethical commitments to racial justice, to the equal rights of every individual, to academic freedom and to the worth of pursuing knowledge and understanding for their own sakes. (To the extent that my conceptions of these basic values conflict with each other, or with the substantive argument within the work, my claims are undermined. I have sought to be consistent.)

Because black people in Britain experience racism as a part of daily life, their voices, sometimes referred to as 'a black perspective', are particularly important in debates about racism and antiracism in education. Why, then, does a white person, as I am, write a book such as this? I believe that white educators can and should undertake antiracist activities, each taking the opportunities to do so afforded by their particular role and responsibilities in the system. My own professional experience, currently as a continuing educator in a university, has generated relevant data and reflection which I can, I hope, usefully share. As a woman of working-class origin, with a daughter who is 'severely disabled', my own personal, daily experience of oppression influences my understanding of it and strengthens a commitment to oppose it in all its forms. Nevertheless, what follows cannot claim to be informed by a black perspective; it comes from a committed (if inadequate) white antiracist.

The book is addressed to students, teachers and policy makers in adult education (and not exclusively university continuing education), to those involved in access developments across post-16 education, to educators concerned with the quality of student learning and to those working with non-standard entry students. It is also intended for those interested and active in higher education *per se*.

I hope it will be of interest to academics researching the topic of 'race' and education, which forms its substance, and to those working in the philosophy of education, which informs my approach.

# Race for a change

The title of the book encapsulates several interrelated claims. *Race for a Change* signifies that ethnicity can, through antiracism, be a force for change; that attention to ethnicity issues, currently very limited, would make a change and that there is good reason (if we value justice) to feel some urgency about securing antiracist changes in both continuing and higher education.

Currently, continuing education (CE) is influencing higher education (HE) (Duke 1992), and there is also a scattering of antiracist practice across university departments (see Chapter 10). An ethically and epistemologically desirable transformation of higher education could be achieved if the latent change power of a more systematic antiracism were combined with a more complete realization of this CE potential. *Together*, antiracism and continuing education would be a more powerful catalyst. Moreover, though singly they could each improve higher education, nevertheless they would produce flawed results. The influence of continuing education without antiracism would give rise to a *racist* version of lifelong higher education; antiracism without the influence of CE would produce a less discriminatory and less ethnocentric version of the competitive finishing school model of HE currently in place.

The structure of the book reflects these claims. Part 1 explicates the notions of continuing education as a change agent, across the university, and, through first changing themselves, continuing education departments as antiracist models for other university departments. In Part 2, the focus shifts from continuing education and CE departmental change and change agency, to higher education and institutional change. What changes would successful, antiracist continuing education produce? In other words, what would antiracist, lifelong higher education be like – at both the departmental and institutional levels?

Chapter 1 begins to explore continuing education as an agent of change and race as a cutting edge in continuing and higher education. Chapters 2 and 3 undertake some conceptual clarification of 'racism' and 'antiracist continuing education'. Though such analysis usually comes first, the less traditional structuring of Part 1 emphasizes the urgency of change and the priority of practical activity to secure it. Chapter 4 focuses on achieving an antiracist university continuing education. Prior to, and as part of, acting as antiracist change agents within the institution, CE departments should themselves practise antiracism. (This priority is logical and ethical, rather than *necessarily* temporal. It is not impossible for academics in departments of continuing education to work simultaneously for change at both levels of the system – departmental and institutional.) Data are provided from a survey identifying examples of CE departmental antiracism and departmental change agency in Chapter 5.

Turning to higher education, Part 2 offers a conception of a university for lifelong learning (Chapter 6). Such an institution would provide better access for mature students, including black students. The issues of access and antiracist outreach are explored in Chapters 7 and 8. Once in the university, these students are entitled to an institution which is sensitive to their needs and interests. In Chapter 9, the (inreach) nature of an antiracist and lifelong higher education is discussed – in relation to research, teaching, curriculum and institutional organization. In the final chapter, current good practice is described. This was identified during a second research project using a questionnaire (see Appendix 3) and follow-up visits, to explore the antiracist activities of a range of university departments. The patchy picture that emerged from this research is contrasted with the vision of a transformed – *antiracist and mature* – university.

# Part 1
# Antiracist Continuing Education: Agent and Model

# 1 | Continuing Education as Change Agent: Inreach and Outreach

## Why change?

There are moral, educational, pragmatic and legal reasons to promote antiracist education at all levels of the system, including higher education. In so far as these reasons are valid, and given that much current university provision and practice is racially discriminatory and ethnocentric, then there are moral, educational, pragmatic and legal reasons why universities should change.

It is not my intention to set out these justifications at great length, since they occur and recur at appropriate points in forthcoming chapters. *Ethical* justifications are implicit in the recurring theme of, and commitment to, equal opportunities for individuals and social groups. Similarly, *educational* justifications for antiracist education arise from the conception of education underpinning notions of continuing education (CE; Chapter 3) and higher education (HE; Chapters 6 and 9). Concern to expand higher education; to increase student numbers, provides *pragmatic* reasons to improve recruitment from minority ethnic groups.

Both principled and pragmatic motivations are discernible as current forces for change in higher education. For example, many teachers involved in access initiatives, such as the development of open college networks, are motivated by equity commitments, and employers and politicians by the need for a better educated workforce. That there are abundant good reasons to work for an expanded higher education is borne out by the many influential, official bodies which have supported the need to improve and increase access to it (see Chapter 8). For this expansion to be antiracist, it must include a greater diversity of clientele, as well as greater numbers – bringing in proportionately more students from currently underrepresented groups.

The requirements of the Race Relations Act 1976, which applies to the whole of the education services of Great Britain (except Northern Ireland),

provide legal reasons for some changes in practice. The Act makes discrimination on grounds of race unlawful. Neither students nor employees
should be subject to such discrimination – in recruitment, promotion,
transfer, conditions of employment, dismissal, training, the provisions of
goods and services, or in the education offered.

Two kinds of discrimination are unlawful: direct and indirect. Direct
racial discrimination consists of treating a person, on racial grounds, less
favourably than others are or would be treated in similar circumstances,
e.g. refusing to employ someone because they are black. 'Racial grounds'
includes race, colour, nationality, citizenship, ethnic or national origins.
Indirect discrimination consists of applying a requirement or condition
which, *intentionally or not*, has a disproportionately adverse effect on a
particular racial group and cannot be justified on non-racial grounds. For
example, word-of-mouth recruitment may exclude black applicants for a
job if the networks and circles of people passing on the information are
all white. Or a qualification may be required (say English GCE) where this
is not relevant and yet tends to disqualify members of minority ethnic
groups. Indirect discrimination is not uncommon and the Commission for
Racial Equality (CRE) and others have successfully taken such cases of
unlawful discrimination to the courts.

Despite these legal requirements, and the principled and pragmatic
forces for antiracist change, in the universities it remains piecemeal and
slow.

## Inreach and outreach

> Departments of Continuing Education should play an important role
> in the development of equal opportunities in their university. Tradi-
> tionally, they have *reached out* beyond the campus to ensure links
> with their local community, and have *reached in* to the university to
> influence the institution's responsiveness specifically to mature stu-
> dents and more generally to the local community at large.
>
> (UCACE 1990: 7)

Given the traditions and values in university continuing education, it is
perhaps not surprising that a recent survey revealed widespread acceptance of the idea of CE departments having a role in promoting antiracist
education within their own institutions (see Chapter 5).

Many departments have sought to influence their university to accept
more mature students. This has involved persuasion towards attitudinal
change and playing a part in the development of new access structures.
They thus have experience of promoting change in values and practice at

the level of the institution. Many departments have a semi-official, and some an official, role in mainstreaming continuing education across the university and have been involved in relevant initiatives, such as the development of part-time degrees. This institutional level activity will have given members of CE departments an understanding of university decision-making procedures, as well as accustoming department and institution to their having a mainstream influence, or even an institution-wide brief. There is already, then, considerable experience of *inreach* work across the university.

Extra-mural and other responsibilities have also ensured that CE departments more than others have kept in touch with local communities. They have conducted informal, and more systematic, market research to discover educational needs and interests, have recruited and trained local people as tutors, and have collaborated with other CE providers and interest groups. Thus they also have considerable experience of *outreach*.

These inreach and outreach activities have partly been motivated by a commitment to equity, which underpins the idea of education as social action, leading to educational initiatives in areas of social deprivation. More pragmatically, the need to find clients to keep up the full-time equivalent has encouraged a culture of enterprise and expansion with a less conservative ethos than is found in many other university departments.

Chris Duke has described this richness of experience as a dowry that university adult education (UAE) brings to its parent institution:

> Let me recall once more the assets of UAE: experience of participation in educational transactions, dialogue, negotiated curriculum, valuing and using students' experience; insights into the experience of curriculum renewal less restricted by the tramlines of departments and their disciplines, more open to other orderings of knowledge derived from life and work experience; a capacity for creating and sustaining external relationships via partnerships, networks, support systems and resource centres; flexibility and lateral thinking in respect of time, place and mode of 'delivery', to bring education to the client, community or organisation on terms and in ways valued and having meaning for the learning partner – the customer or consumer.
>
> (Duke 1988: 13)

All of these factors – values, traditions and experience – suggest that CE departments have the potential to be effective agents for antiracist change in higher education: reaching into their universities to mainstream antiracist curricula and structures, and reaching out to local minority ethnic groups.

In order to promote antiracism, departments must of course also develop their own curricula and departmental decision-making structures;

that is, they must practise before they preach. Such departments will provide an example of good practice for well-disposed colleagues in other departments. University innovations which are internal in origin are more likely to be successful when they thus focus on the 'operational mode' and influence values through changes in practice (Mathias *et al.* 1986).

Because CE departments are firmly on the inside of the institution and yet have outreach experience, they are in a good position to act as a channel for external pressures, perceptions and expertise. Their liaison, collaboration and dialogue with local minority ethnic groups will enhance their own work but could also be part of a more institution-wide process. We know that university innovations which are primarily external in origin are likely to be more successful if based on value considerations – the 'normative mode' (Mathias *et al.* 1986). University responsiveness to such external pressures is at least partly based on value considerations about equity.

The likelihood of success in antiracist innovation is enhanced if conscious attention is given to the process of change and to the local politics of race. Some academics in CE departments have studied institutional change in one form or another and have some understanding of the factors that bear on the success or failure of CE initiatives – an understanding which could be applied to antiracist change. In turn, experience of the nature and politics of antiracist innovation at first hand, together with reflection on it, will add to that existing understanding of institutional change.

## The politics of institutional change

Power in universities is widely distributed, with considerable autonomy at all levels of the system: central administration, department and individual academic. Because departments are the 'basic unit', they are one of the most powerful influences for change (Mathias *et al.* 1986). Due to the diffuse nature of decision making, which relies on a complex committee structure[1]* with debate and dissent, the process of change is likely to be convoluted, piecemeal and slow but, looked at more optimistically, can be worked for and achieved at different levels and be strongly influenced by departmental activity.

Those factors which have been identified as decisive in a change process include gain and loss, ownership, leadership and power (Mathias *et al.* 1986). Antiracist development provides considerable gain in the form of satisfaction through the realization of a commitment to equality and, ultimately I shall argue, in terms of the enhancement of the central

* Superscript numerals refer to numbered notes at the end of the book.

academic tasks. Ownership of the change is important – hence the emphasis in race relations on wide involvement and consultation in the construction of policy or action plans. Leadership, in the sense of support from central and departmental formal leaders, combined with informal leadership from those introducing the innovation, has a significant bearing on success. Neither 'top down' injunction nor 'bottom up' activism are as effective as the collaborative, shared leadership model. Nevertheless, pressures and incentives backed by formal power are also conducive to change.

In the race relations field, research has identified three factors which have influenced local authority development of equal opportunities: spontaneous protest, pressure for community resources and planned political struggle (Ben Tovin *et al.* 1986). And three further influencing themes: corporate action, co-option and consultation (Ball 1987). Given that universities are, like local authorities, complex organizations with diffuse power structures, there may be lessons to be learned from this. If protest and community pressure have been significant factors for local education authority developments, then the university will be less likely to change if protected from this by its ivory walls. Departments of continuing education could on occasions bring key university leaders and committees face to face with local minority anger on various issues. Individuals from departments can also identify likely corporate bodies, such as the Association of University Teachers (AUT) and the students' union, with whom to work for antiracist change. In those universities which do not yet have them, it is useful to work for the establishment of equal opportunities officers and units, and an equal opportunities committee. Through co-option and consultation, black individuals and representatives of local minority ethnic organizations can participate in university decision making which may also lead to a stronger voice for black people in the new structures and procedures which emerge.

## Changes and the contemporary scene

Demographic and economic trends are currently encouraging changes in higher education. These changes *may* lead to a more diverse clientele. Without real efforts to counter racism, however, such change could be worthwhile for various 'non-traditional' students or 'deprived' social groups, yet leave black people on the outside. Therefore, CE departments, as participants in the changes to widen access, to democratize decision making, to develop pedagogy and the curriculum, to provide better pastoral support and problematize existing selection and assessment criteria, have a responsibility to ensure that race issues are a part of all this.

That there is considerable pressure for relatively rapid change in higher education seems generally agreed. Thus Parry and Wake (1990), for example, describe the 1980s as 'a decade of pressure to widen access' and the Organization for Economic Cooperation and Development (OECD 1983) talks of the 'crisis of higher education', requiring 'a re-appraisal of the special position of the university'. In order to ensure that contemporary movements in higher education will have antiracist outcomes, university adult educators, in their inreach and outreach initiatives, must incorporate antiracism as an effective cutting edge.

## Race as a cutting edge

In a note to this chapter,[2] I briefly describe the influence of race and culture issues during three decades of development in education. Though there was less change in higher education than in other sectors, as a proven catalyst for change in schools, and used in conjunction with the inreach and outreach dowry of university continuing education, antiracism provides a potentially powerful cutting edge through which universities *could* be transformed. In what follows, I briefly unpack those elements inherent in antiracism, in which its change potential consists.

The potential transformative power of antiracism derives from several sources. First, as was indicated, political and ethical factors come into play. The sense of current injustice in an arena that prides itself on equality of opportunity and reward based on merit fuels pressures of various kinds. Second, there are educational factors. Once antiracism and education are coupled, new and fruitful learning opportunities are born. Incorporating a variety of cultural traditions enriches the curriculum; generating antiracist change creates an opportunity for learning through social action; and to develop an awareness of racist assumptions, biases and stereotyping (in the media, for example) is an effective means of sharpening the learner's critical skills.

The *variety* of established *cultural* traditions (religions, languages, art forms, etc.) is readily perceived by educators as a means to generate enriched meaning perspectives for learners (Mezirow 1977) and as a source of additional curriculum materials for teachers. Although other oppressed groups have forms of experience that enrich our collective knowledge, as Carol Gilligan's (1982) gender-related research enriched our understanding of moral development, the epistemological potential of these other oppressed perspectives is more easily overlooked than that of cultural diversity. Moreover, the development of a *pluralist curriculum*, which may be more readily seen by the more conservative as directly relevant to education and less threatening than *structural* change, has, nevertheless, sometimes spearheaded antiracist structural changes.

In addition, race acts as a barium meal in the system. Showing how institutions discriminate against black people makes clear where power lies and how decisions are made. The hidden or taken-for-granted institutional structures become visible. We can thus recognize where discretionary judgements could be influenced by racial prejudice and how institutional practices discriminate directly and indirectly. We can see how these practices embody different forms of discrimination: hidden or overt, deliberate or unconscious, tacitly acknowledged but disguised. Showing up (in both senses of the term) the key structures in the functioning of an institution has the advantage of pointing up the features which should be changed. In a sense, this makes concrete what might otherwise remain a nebulous vision of equality. By understanding racism in action, within the structural skeleton and below the surface of the institution's service skin, we can see in detail the stark contrast between what is and what could be, and we are provided with concrete and achievable objectives towards our goal of equality.

Moreover, recognizing racism can also help us to understand more about the nature of oppression in education and sharpen our awareness in relation to other oppressed groups (the unemployed, women, the aged, people with disabilities, gays, etc.). It therefore has the potential to set in train changes that will benefit many social groups, leading ultimately to a radically different provision.

# 2 | Conceptual Clarification: 'Racism' and 'Antiracist Education'

Before turning to antiracist continuing education in practice, I want to look more closely at key relevant concepts, particularly 'racism', 'antiracist education' and 'antiracist continuing education'.

## 'Racism' and 'antiracist education'

'Racism' is a many-stranded term that has been used to refer to different (although related) kinds of social phenomena. It is sometimes used to refer to beliefs about genetic inferiority, and sometimes to actions, including both deliberate and unintentional racial discrimination whether or not that discrimination is accompanied by these kinds of belief. Similarly, the adjective 'racist' has been applied to people, to beliefs, to actions by individuals and to institutional practices and procedures. There are even said to be different forms of racism within the same category of phenomena and it will be useful to clarify which ones are relevant to education and how they are relevant.

'Race' itself is a purely social categorization of people based on the tendency of some physical characteristics to be distinguishable. There are no important biological differences between ethnic groups. Some people put the term race in quotation marks to show its social rather than its scientific significance. The social significance of race itself rests on the reality of different forms of racism. In other words, whereas the naive (and racist) assumption is that the scientific reality of race gives rise to the phenomenon of racism, the racial categorization is actually only significant and perpetuated because of racism. (Cultural differences are more 'real' than so-called racial ones and raise more difficult issues.) One explanatory slogan about racism which has been widely used by antiracist educators is:

$$\text{Prejudice} + \text{Power} = \text{Racism}$$

The message encapsulated is that racism occurs when a racially pre-judiced individual or group has the power to act out that prejudice in a harmful discriminatory action. This is the basis of the claim that in Britain only white people can be racist. Although individual black people can indeed be prejudiced against whites, it is because the dominant white group has the power to discriminate so systematically against members of the less powerful groups, that significant racially based social, economic and educational disadvantage occurs.

It is African-Caribbean and Asian people who most experience this racial discrimination and disadvantage and I am using 'black' to refer (but not necessarily exclusively) to both groups. There is much discussion and disagreement about the appropriateness of the term, which is a political rather than a descriptive label. Some black people (in this political sense) have a lighter skin tone than some white Europeans. My use of 'black' is based on preferring it to various alternatives (e.g. 'coloured' has colonial connotations and in any case we are all some skin tone or another). The use of 'black', however, is not meant to imply that racism is always about colour. Prejudice and discrimination based on colour is prevalent, but it is not the whole story. Madood (1992) has called it the 'ground floor of the building' of racism, which has other levels, including prejudice and discrimination based on culture and ethnicity. Incidentally, 'ethnic minority group' sounds as though only minority groups are ethnic. 'Minority ethnic group', though rather cumbersome, at least indicates that there is a majority ethnic group too.

Prejudice, the first term in the slogan, is often described as a preconceived opinion or bias for or against someone or something where the opinion has been formed without adequate information on which to base a rational judgement. Such judgements are often directed against groups of people who are assumed to share common attributes and behaviour patterns. Racial prejudice thus requires one to form a stereotype of a particular group of people which then allows one to judge a member of that group according to an established set of expectations. Thus the two factors that are necessary for racial prejudice initially to be formed and maintained, are ignorance and the existence of stereotypes of particular groups of people. These stereotypes are reinforced by the media and by the education process. Interesting research by van Dijk (1987) has demonstrated that the *same* stereotypes directed against *different* minorities are perpetuated in talk and thought across several European countries.

Because in Britain there are different (as well as some overlapping) stereotypes of African-Caribbean and Asian groups (Madood 1991), this may be one of the reasons why racism manifests itself in different forms in relation to each group. Thus African-Caribbeans are stereotypically held to be more aggressive than Asians and it is the supposedly more passive

Asians who most suffer racist attacks. Because African-Caribbeans are held to be less hard working and intelligent than Asians, they have faired less well in terms of teacher expectations and educational assessments.

Prejudice rests on beliefs which are irrational because there is an *emotional* resistance to changing them in the light of new evidence. Indeed, the evidence is distorted to fit the prejudice. As the slogan implies, prejudices do tend to be exhibited in action; in the case of racial prejudices, these will be discriminatory actions by which a person is unfairly treated because of belonging to a particular racial group rather than another, more favourably treated one. It is a matter of fact that prejudice tends to be exhibited in progressively more harmful discrimination (Allport 1958). It is a matter of logic that we could not have the concept of prejudice if it were not normally exhibited in publicly observable behaviour.

This characterization of racism as power-backed prejudice leading to discriminatory actions can be distinguished from *institutional racism*, although this is also seen as important by antiracist educators. Institutional racism is distinct from prejudiced power in that it does not involve individuals *qua* individuals with prejudices, but individuals *qua* individuals as functionaries of an institution, and need not involve prejudicial intentions at all. The Swann Report (1985) defined it as the way in which a range of long-established systems, practices and procedures in education and the wider society, which were originally devised to meet the needs of a relatively homogeneous society, may unintentionally work against minority groups by depriving them of opportunities open to the majority population. The significant point about this conception is that it draws attention to structures and processes within institutions that are harmful in their effect.

It is *outcome* rather than *intention* that is important. And, obviously, not just any outcome justifies the description 'institutional racism', but outcomes which are harmful to members of a particular racial group or groups because they disadvantage these people *qua* members of those groups relative to members of some other racial group or groups. Practices which work against relative interests in this way may be seen as unfair.

These harmful outcomes can arise through passive or active forms of behaviour – 'failing to take account of' or 'actively working against'. The Swann Report (1985) gives two examples: arrangements for electing governors may fail to take account of the need for minority ethnic group representatives; and the provision of *separate* language schools for children whose first language is not English may actively work against their interests. (This is reminiscent of the Race Relations Act distinction between indirect and direct discrimination.)

It is a widespread disadvantage in matters that affect the quality of one's life that connects the notion of institutional practices with the notion of injustice. Those cases of discrimination in which either there was no harm done or the notion of unfairness was irrelevant, would not be cases of institutional racism. Institutions often do discriminate without harm. For example, hospitals provide anti-malaria injections only to people intending to travel to certain parts of the world. I have not, however, found it possible to think of an example of harmful *racial* discrimination which could be said to be fair.

Examples of institutional racism include:

1. 'Word-of-mouth recruitment'. A particular example is the 'lads of dads' syndrome in companies which offer their apprenticeships to the sons and nephews of the existing skilled, white workforce (Lee and Wrench 1983). There is no deliberate intention to exclude black youngsters perhaps, but the result, nevertheless, is that they do not have the opportunity to acquire a trade.
2. People who do not speak English are gravely disadvantaged in hospitals with monolingual doctors which fail to provide appropriate interpreters.
3. Many assessment procedures and tests are culturally biased. Thus the abilities of students who are not members of the dominant cultural group may be misassessed.

Of course, even where the discrimination is unintentional, the prevalence of racial prejudice is not necessarily irrelevant. When the harmful consequences of some unintended discriminations are pointed out, there is often a reluctance to change the practices in question. The degree of resistance to change seems to me to be related both to endemic prejudices and to an unwillingness to relinquish power.

White people have established the relevant procedures and the relevant criteria and implement these at key points. On the whole, they are the employers, they sit on interview panels, write references, assess ability and so on. They hold the institutionally authorized positions such as justice of the peace, judge, headteacher, housing officer and bank manager, through which the quality of people's lives may be affected. White people in the main also form the government and, even within a parliamentary democracy, insufficient constitutional protection of human rights leaves vulnerable those minorities which might be unjustly treated by the elected body.

To extend the earlier definition in line with these considerations, institutional racism occurs when the power of a racially prejudiced dominant group legitimates the carrying out of institutional practices which, sometimes intentionally and more often unintentionally, discriminate unjustly and to the detriment of members of minority ethnic groups. One could, of course, describe unwitting discrimination simply as 'institutional discrimination' and reserve the harsher term 'institutional racism' for cases of deliberate discrimination. However, this would ignore the important point that, in terms of the lives of black people, it is the harmful *outcomes* of institutional procedures, and not the *intentions* of the people who happen to be involved, which is important.

Given this phenomenon of institutional racism, it is clear that there are complex questions to be raised about our responsibilities in relation to it (Leicester 1988). We are not just responsible for what we do, but also for what we fail to do. Failure to act in relation to institutional racism preserves the inegalitarian *status quo*. Clearly, if I have some responsibility for the functioning of a particular institution, then I have some direct responsibility for how justly or unjustly it delivers its services. And the greater my power and influence within the institution, the greater my responsibility tends to be.

So far, we have considered individual and institutional racism. Todd (1991) describes these as different levels of analysis and adds a third level, 'structural racism', which is concerned with the broader and historically embedded patterns of social inequality. In practice, the phenomena described by the three levels of analysis are interconnected. Teacher expectations of black students can influence their performance; poorer performance may be the uncritical basis of decision making about streaming in schools or entry to higher-level courses post-school. These decisions perpetuate underachievement. A disproportionate concentration of minority ethnic students in lower streams or on less academic courses has its broader effect in strengthening historically embedded patterns of socio-economic inequality.

Halstead (1988) distinguishes between six types of racism: pre-reflective gut racism (emotional and deeply entrenched prejudice); post-reflective gut racism (ideology of racial superiority and domination); institutional racism (as previously defined); paternalistic racism (well-intentioned regulations drawn up by whites); colour-blind racism (treating people the same, based on ethnocentric assumptions about what that treatment should be like); and cultural racism in which the focal point of prejudice and discrimination are cultural rather than racial characteristics.

Cultural racism involves seeing the cultural traditions of minority groups as flawed and threatening and demands cultural conformity to dominant group norms. It could be contrasted with pluralism, by which is meant more than the mere fact of ethnic diversity. Pluralism implies the valuing of such diversity, and the principle of equality of treatment for these various groups. (In my view, cultural racism is currently increasing, against Muslims in particular.)

Halstead suggests that racial injustice is what all six forms of racism have in common and that understanding racism as injustice has several advantages. It relates the problem of racism to a fundamental value about which we should all be concerned, is not linked to a particular political theory and provides a framework (the principles of justice) within which it can be discussed. I would support this in that the most important thing, in terms of the quality of life for black people, is to change the disadvantaging outcome of all the kinds of phenomena called 'racist'. It is *inequitable outcomes* that constitute the unifying link between all these forms, levels and types of racism, and the notion of inequitable outcomes is related to the idea of injustice. Inequality of opportunity is unfair and leads to inequitable outcomes.

The philosopher Anthony Flew has argued that there is not necessarily a connection between equality of opportunity and equality of outcome: that the absence of the latter does not entail the absence of the former. This is logically correct in a formal sense. There is no *logical* connection between inequality of outcome and opportunity. Nevertheless, as a matter of fact, inequality of outcome for racial groups is a good indication that there is indeed inequality of opportunity through some form of racial discrimination – often subtle, indirect or unintentional. Black people are not inherently less able than whites. Any situation of racial disadvantage therefore warrants scrutiny and, if we value justice, usually requires remedy through change. Antiracism, as the opposition to all forms of racism, could be explicated in terms of actions to change the unfair features of any situation which results in racial disadvantage.

Antiracism in education will therefore involve opposition to all three levels of racism: individual, institutional and in the system as a whole. Since prejudice is learned and the education process is an important element in that learning, an antiracist curriculum will seek to develop the critical skills to discern racial bias in what is presented in non-formal and formal educational contexts. Adult education would intend students to achieve a level of critical awareness that encouraged an antiracist commitment. Such 'teaching' to raise awareness of racism will include direct work about race relations where appropriate but would more commonly be part of other studies (e.g. media, cultural or women's studies, literature, sociology, philosophy, and so on). In continuing education, there is currently much discussion about education for citizenship. The *good* citizen (in the form of college governor or whatever) presumably implies, among other things, the commitment and skill to fulfil one's functions justly; through fair employment practice, for instance.

Antiracism outside the classroom involves opposing institutional racism. The contradiction between antiracist work at seminar level within an institution that does not embody fair practice in its own procedures is a commonplace anomaly.

'Antiracism in education' has been both joined to and contrasted with 'multicultural education'; the latter being perhaps the more widely used term (see Chapter 10). Multicultural education places emphasis on cultural issues in education rather than on antiracism. 'Multicultural education' implies that the education process makes use of worthwhile knowledge from several cultural traditions and places value on developing values, knowledge, understanding and skills appropriate to a pluralist society. Parekh, who has written extensively and persuasively about the value of multicultural education, sums it up thus:

> The inspiring principle of multicultural education then is to sensitize the child [*sic*] to the inherent plurality of the world – the plurality of systems, beliefs, ways of life, cultures, modes of analysing familiar experiences, ways of looking at historical events, and so on.
>
> (Parekh 1986: 27)

# 3 | Conceptual Clarification: 'Antiracist Continuing Education'

How are influential notions of continuing education affected by the antiracist ideal? To bypass terminological quibbles about whether we should use 'continuing education' or 'adult education', etc., I shall simply concentrate on widely shared guiding assumptions and aims: that continuing education involves a conception of education as lifelong, rather than a 'front end' model which equates education with schooling; that, notwithstanding its involvement in practice with vocational courses, it is in the tradition of liberal education and is concerned to establish what might be distinctive of the adult stage of this; and that it is also associated with ideas about 'education for social change'. Thus, by means of an antiracist analysis of these key ideas – lifelong education, liberal education and social action – I intend to throw light on what might be meant by an 'antiracist continuing education'.

Adult educators tend, implicitly at least, to see education as an open-ended process, not a final state attainable at some particular point in a person's life at which they become 'educated'. As Wain (1984) has pointed out, this is not to deny the existence or distinctiveness of an upbringing stage within the process. It is, however, to accept that post-school education is a necessary and distinct aspect of full individual and social development.

Wain's justification for the 'lifelong' concept is a pragmatic one, resting on psychological, vocational and political pressures on people living in modern technological societies. I would add that the kinds of processes involved in education are inherently open-ended (Leicester 1988). Education in a culturally plural society (and all that implies in additional cognitive, affective, behavioural and social objectives) might be thought to be even more obviously a lifelong matter.

In adulthood, persons continue to learn from their experience and to integrate this into increasingly comprehensive perspectives. (By perspective I mean the evolving cognitive framework which incorporates the concepts, beliefs, values, interests and emotions through which one comprehends the world.) These perspectives are modified to make better sense of a growing range of experiences. Some adult educators have conceived of education in relation to these perspectives. S.D. Brookfield, for example, says that effective facilitation of adult learning involves challenging learners to examine their previously held values, beliefs and behaviour, and confronting them with perspectives of the world which diverge from those they already hold. He suggests that adult education is not a matter of aquiring a set of fixed competences but a process of lifelong learning through a praxis of continual reflection and action (Brookfield 1986). Similarly, Mezirow sees adult education in terms of the kind of learning that involves becoming critically aware of the cultural and psychological assumptions that influence the way we pattern our lives. He calls this learning about 'meaning perspectives' (Mezirow 1977).

We have a natural tendency to make sense of our experience. This is to make meaning – to construct an interpretation of experience which we use to guide action. In making experience meaningful, we employ a conceptual scheme – a structure of categorical concepts, interpretive principles and truth criteria into which we are initiated as children. More sophisticated learning takes place when a dissonant experience ('a disorienting dilemma') leads us to reflect critically on and evaluate the sociocultural presuppositions of our conceptual schema and in so doing to change it in order to integrate the new experience with our previous experience. This is a process of individual development which can be deliberately facilitated by the educator to assist the learner into ever more finely discriminating and integrated conceptual schemes.

Mezirow's account of 'perspective transformation' as a distinctively adult domain of learning is a more fully worked out description of this meaning-making of human beings; an account which he derives from Habermas's theory of knowledge. For Habermas (Thompson 1981), human interest generates knowledge in three generic areas. One of these is the 'emancipatory area', in which interest in self-knowledge has generated the social sciences. Mezirow applies this to the individual adult learner, who undergoes an emancipatory process of becoming critically aware of how one's meaning perspective structures experience and how, through reflection, one transforms the perspective to assimilate new experience. He defines 'meaning perspective' as the structure of assumptions that constitutes a frame of reference for interpreting the meaning of an experience, 'reflection' as the examination of the justification for one's beliefs, primarily to guide action; and 'critical reflection' as the assessment of the validity of the presuppositions of one's meaning perspectives and examination of their sources and consequences (Mezirow 1990). Emancipatory education is an organized effort to precipitate or to facilitate the student's reformulation of a meaning perspective to allow a more inclusive, discriminatory and integrative understanding of one's experience. For Mezirow, learning includes acting on these new insights.

This natural process of individual development or learning is an *educative* process in that it leads to *superior* perspectives – that is, perspectives better able to make sense of more and different experiences. In formal education, the learner and 'teacher' engage in 'critical discourse' to arrive at a consensual assessment of the justification of an idea. (Intersubjective agreement provides an objective reference point in a subjective process.) When meaning perspectives evolve through collective critical reflection as in the women's movement, says Mezirow, then *shared* meaning is generated. Mezirow's reference to this collective process could also be seen as a brief account of the construction of objective knowledge, similar in some respects to Popperian 'objective knowledge' in that it evolves and is tested over time, is intersubjectively agreed and in the public domain. It is interesting to reflect on the relationship between the meaning perspectives of private individuals and the construction of shared knowledge in the public domain. Presumably, not only does knowledge in the public domain arise through collective critical reflection (as in the women's movement), but also is added to and sometimes transformed (as with Kuhn's 'paradigm shifts' in natural science) through contributions from powerful elements in an individual's meaning perspective which can resolve anomalies in the currently accepted collective knowledge and which are sufficiently fruitful to acquire widespread consent.

Mezirow's influential work in adult education is directly relevant to 'antiracist continuing education'. He sees adulthood as the time for reassessing those assumptions of one's formative years which have resulted in distorted views of reality. Most school leavers finish their schooling with deeply racist assumptions. The adult educator's task is 'helping the learner identify real problems involving reified power relationships rooted in institutionalised ideologies which one has internalised in one's psychological history' (Mezirow 1983). Moreover, Mezirow (1990) points out that the 'disorienting dilemma' triggering the transformation process may be evoked by one's efforts to understand a different culture that challenges one's presuppositions.

In Mezirow's (1990) collection *Fostering Critical Reflection in Adulthood*, W.B. Kennedy describes how critical reflection on racism, sexism and classism can be fostered through an analysis of meaning perspectives in formal educational settings.

According to Mezirow's theory, the distortions in our meaning perspectives may be either epistemic, socio-cultural or psychic. Two of these are readily discernible in racist ideology and the third inhibits antiracist action. Thus the epistemic distortion of reification (seeing a phenomenon produced by social interaction as immutable and beyond human control) strongly influences racist assumptions about 'deprived' groups, leading to the pathologizing of black people. Rather than having problems, they are seen as the problem. The socio-cultural distortions involve taking for granted belief systems that pertain to power and social relationships, especially those currently prevailing and legitimized and enforced by institutions. A common socio-cultural distortion is mistaking self-fulfilling and self-validating beliefs for those that are not, as with stereotyping and the criminalization of black youth. Psychic distortions have to do with presuppositions generating unwarranted anxiety that impedes taking action. (Mezirow cites psychiatrist Roger Gould's theory that traumatic events in childhood can result in parental prohibitions that although submerged from consciousness continue to inhibit adult action by generating anxiety feelings where there is a risk of breaching them.) The anxiety results in a lost function, such as the ability to confront, a necessary ingredient in antiracist activity.

Mezirow's perspective transformation is in the tradition of liberal education, which conceives of education as liberating the learner through the development of a rational mind. The development of a rational mind involves – some would say is equivalent to (Hirst 1965) – the acquisition of certain sorts of knowledge. These liberating forms of knowledge generate understanding and are therefore of intrinsic value.

Bailey (1984) has described liberal education as being characterized by:

1. Its capacity to liberate a person from the restrictions of the present and the particular.
2. Its involvement of the learner in what is most fundamental and general.
3. Its involvement of the learner in intrinsically worthwhile ends.
4. Its involvement of the learner in reason and the development of the rational mind.

Bailey points out that to ask why we should develop reason already presupposes a commitment to it. However, unlike some philosophers who appeal to this kind of transcendental deduction (e.g. Peters 1966), he does not suppose that it establishes that education must have the development of rationality as its central objective. Accordingly, Bailey produces supplementary instrumental and ethical arguments in favour of liberal education.

An education which emphasizes the development of rational belief is inherently anti-prejudice. It also accords a kind of protection of minority viewpoints and lifestyles in that it encourages tolerance of difference – valuing debate and persuasion above the imposition of a dominant orthodoxy.

However, liberal education, including Mezirow's perspective transformation, is thought by some to place too great an emphasis on individual development and the individual learner rather than on what could be seen as a less selfish and less narcissistic emphasis on community development and collective learning through social change. The idea of education as social action is the idea that we can recognize and change current power structures using the change process as a collective learning experience for those involved. This places the emphasis on community-based education and on experiential learning through critical reflection on action.

Education has potential either to maintain the *status quo* or to initiate social change. In the first paradigm, the university offers courses to the elite and perhaps to selected individuals from 'deprived' groups. In the second, educator and oppressed learn together as they promote social action against oppression, sharing power in relation to the change agenda and the learning process involved.

In the same Mezirow (1990) collection mentioned previously, Heaney and Horton provide a chapter on 'Reflective engagement for social change'. Their example of learning through social action began with a 1960 student sit-in at Highlander Folk School, Tennessee. This had a major transformative effect on the participants and on the civil rights movement of the southern states. The director and staff of this adult education centre emphasized that they were there to help students to do what they (the students) decided to do.

Liberal education can neglect social empowerment; individuals can change their perspectives without affecting their ability to change the *status quo*. On the other hand, adult educators sometimes talk and write about 'education as social action' in a way that reifies the collective and overlooks the fact that it is individuals (and *only* individuals) who can learn. Moreover, there is something a little odd about (highly qualified) university educators inveighing against (selfish) individual development. It is because individual learning is generated by the social action that such activity is a species of *education*. Without this, social action to ameliorate the oppression of an individual would be indistinguishable from social work, and social action to ameliorate the oppression of a social group would simply be political activity. The educator involves individual learners in a process which is simultaneously one of learning and of social change. It is this which distinguishes her from the social worker and the political activist. Heaney and Horton point out that Freire's 'conscientization' involves critical self-reflection *and* transformative action. Conscientization involves an individual's recognition of hidden dimensions of our reality through reflective engagement in resisting oppressions. Thus both critical reflection (individual learning) and transformative action are essentially linked. This kind of empowering education reconciles the two traditions

– liberal and social action – and does so in such a manner that anti-oppression is the keystone.

There is a broad range of oppressed social groups whose situation could be addressed through education as social action. When such activity is directed at the education system itself, it is often generated by activists for 'equal opportunities' in education. Severe, systematic and disadvantaging discrimination is experienced by the unemployed, by women, by gays, by people with disabilities and by other social groups. At the level of daily experience, such oppression is felt as a severe loss of choice, with adverse effects on the quality of one's life. Education which combined liberal objectives of individual development with radical concern to transform oppressive structures would involve collective action such that this action provided a learning experience for its participants *and* brought about anti-oppressive social change. Suppose, for example, a black voluntary organization becomes aware that black people in a locality are receiving less favourable housing allocation by the local authority. Adult educators could collaborate with that organization to research the process generating this discrimination and to decide on and implement a strategy to end it. This is distinguishable from simple political activity in that educators and learners accept that individual learning is an objective within the process and that the educators have some responsibility to facilitate this – by, for instance, organizing sessions for collective reflection before and after each stage of the process and by making available existing relevant knowledge and expertise.

I have dwelt at some length on influential ideas about continuing education, ideas which presuppose education's 'lifelong' orientation and which reflect its liberal and social foundations. I have done so in order to show that antiracist education, far from being an adjunct to or icing on the cake of continuing education, is an instrinsic part of what it is widely seen to be about. Whether continuing education is conceptualized in terms of perspective transformation or social action or individual *and* social empowerment, emancipation from oppression is an integral part. Thus it becomes a matter of logic (as well as of values) that continuing education be antiracist. To be antiracist is part of what 'continuing education' means.

Given these ideals about antiracist continuing education, in what follows I shall examine how they can be put into practice, what strategies can be used, and what departments of continuing education are actually doing (1) to further develop their own antiracist practice and (2) as antiracist change agents university-wide.

# 4 | Practising What We Preach: Departmental Change

## Departmental antiracism

I have suggested that departments of continuing education could act as change agents – developing antiracist education across their university and incorporating an antiracist cutting edge to their 'mainstreaming' of continuing education. Additionally and simultaneously, departments should be actively internalizing antiracism: at the level of student learning (e.g. teaching methodology, teacher attitudes and expectations, learning resources, the curriculum, student assessment) and at the level of departmental structures – the policies and practices which, intentionally or unintentionally, discriminate against minority ethnic groups (e.g. policies and processes of staff and student recruitment and selection, procedures for dealing with racist incidents, the criteria and practices for staff promotion or training). In developing departmental antiracism, two kinds of educational provisions must be considered: first, provision to meet the so-called 'special needs' of minority ethnic group students and, second, mainstream provision for all students.

The term 'special needs' is not used in this context in the way that it is in the 1981 Education Act concerning special education. There it is concerned with the concept of learning difficulty. [Incidentally, some black students have been wrongly thought to be less able than they are because what has been assessed is not their learning ability or conceptual level but simply their competence in standard English (Coard 1981).] The term should be used with caution (warranting my quotation marks) because the so-called special needs of minority ethnic group students are not special at all, but the same linguistic and cultural educational needs of any student in this society (to learn English, for example). To meet these 'same needs' may require additional or different provision (e.g. English taught as a second language). Catering for the special needs of minority ethnic group students is thus about *additional or different provision.*[1]

The second kind of educational provision involves recognizing that to be educated in and for a multicultural society has implications for the mainstream curriculum, i.e. for the education of all. This stems from a more radical perspective on education and ethnic diversity which involves a re-orientation (Mullard 1984) of our thinking, with extensive implications. For example, the curriculum development task of eliminating ethnocentricity from what is taught should be undertaken in every programme, across the entire curriculum, thus transforming the syllabus for CertEd, MEd, extramural and professional/industrial courses.

In seeking to promote departmental antiracism, some or all of the following obstacles may hinder progress: inertia; resource limitations of time, energy and money; an inherently conservative institution; the entrenched power of the departmental hierarchy; and the weight of established ways of doing things. (Unfortunately, recent legislation has also made antiracist continuing education more difficult to practise or achieve.[2])

## Strategies for departmental change

What general principles could guide CE departmental development of antiracist education and what are the implications of these for specific areas of work? Initially, the issue of racial equality has to be raised sufficiently forcefully and often to ensure that it gets on to the department's agenda – ideally leading to the construction of a departmental action plan. Often, antiracist initiatives are the projects of specific individuals, and to advance from a patchwork of individual initiatives (however worthwhile in themselves) entails finding ways of embedding them, wherever possible, into the organizational structures of the department, including its resource policy. It follows from the preceding discussion that development is required at the structural and curriculum levels and that the curriculum includes 'special needs' and 'education for all'. Since racism is many-faceted, it follows that antiracism must be so too.

The general ethos of the department is a particularly significant factor. Relatively less hierarchical and less closed decision-making procedures discourage patronage and ensure that no single individual is acting out of (possibly unconscious) bias. To achieve democratization requires that 'senior' people in the department are prepared to share power which, at some point and however subtle, is always used (saints excepted!) to privilege self and favoured others. It is partly because democratization entails that the currently most influential people lose some of this privilege and power that institutional racism is difficult to dismantle.

Open discussion and consensus decision making ensure that all points of view can be heard. Ideally, the department should find ways of ensuring that *all* relevant voices are included: student and local community representation, for example. Where a representative is to serve on a particular departmental committee, the relevant group should of course choose their own representative (women staff for female representation; the community group itself for community representation; members of the course for student representation; etc.). The familiar scenario of white people choosing black representation (usually in tokenistic quantity) is racist.

The quality of interpersonal relations (collaborative or competitive, supportive or sniping) contributes to whether the department tends to be inclusive or exclusive in orientation. (Ironically, exclusive 'antiracist' or 'feminist' cliques are not uncommon.) A good departmental ethos will be manifested in several forms of non-oppression: provision of creche facilities, no unnecessary division between academic and support staff, provision for people with disabilities, and so on.

There is sometimes empty rhetoric and lip service paid to antiracism and equal opportunities. This is particularly likely to occur in areas like continuing education which have a liberal, progressive, democratic tradition. For example, there may be a structure of apparently consensual meetings, with the real decisions being taken elsewhere; or the inclusion of support staff in meetings which are not particularly conducive to real participation, while excluding them from decisions of consultation about matters affecting their work. (The 'macho' style of leadership is thus racist as well as sexist.)

One of the first steps for a department that seriously intends to further develop antiracist education is the construction and adoption of an antiracist policy statement. For some, this may be part of a broader equal opportunities policy. Although in themselves policy statements change nothing, they can be a trigger for action and provide support and justification for antiracist initiatives. Good policy statements will go beyond statements of principle to include practical guidance about implementing these principles with recommendations, including attention to ways of resourcing antiracist initiatives and monitoring their effectiveness. (Current attention to quality in adult continuing education, which was the theme of the April 1992 UCACE annual conference, should include the monitoring of antiracist initiatives: their effectiveness in achieving planned objectives, the educational quality of the objectives attained and their contribution to equitable change.)

The process of constructing a policy provides a learning experience for those involved. The working group should include black individuals and representatives of minority organizations, support as well as academic staff, and student representation; it should consult widely and incorporate an open discussion session on an early draft. Antiracism, in terms of activities to produce relevant change, is often an antiracist learning experience for those involved – an example of in-house 'education as social action'.

An antiracist or equal opportunities awareness course for all departmental staff would also be a useful early activity. Department staff should not, of course, be understood to refer only to full-time academics, but to all who work for the department – full- or part-time, temporary or tenured, support, administrative or academic.

Such racism awareness courses have been widely criticized. Some on the political right have claimed that they are left-wing indoctrination; others on the left, that they amount to guilt-inducing indulgence which changes nothing. A good course, however, will increase awareness of personal racism and understanding of the nature of prejudice and racism, combined with developing skills and commitment relevant to antiracist change. And a *departmental* course provides the opportunity to think collectively about the implementation of antiracism in each specific area of the department's work (for a model introductory short course, see Leicester 1989b: 94–101).

As adult educators, we have an obvious responsibility to ensure our own continuing education. White teachers need to be open to a black perspective, by which I mean the views of those who experience the injustice of racial discrimination on a daily basis. One will be particularly interested in books and talks on antiracist education by black authors, documentaries by black producers and the views of black students and colleagues.

There are disproportionately few black members of staff at all levels in universities. Appointment procedures should be reviewed. Word-of-mouth recruitment, for example, is racist because it disadvantages groups outside the current white university network. All posts should be widely advertised, including in the minority press.

Selection criteria for academic staff should include a demonstration of appropriate knowledge and experience to develop an antiracist and pluralist curriculum. Departments of adult and continuing education often need to make short-term appointments quickly, and may lose some of the contract time if an almost immediate starting date cannot be achieved. To cover this situation, departments need to work out a non-racist strategy for quick appointments which yet avoids patronage or tapping the white network. They could, for instance, develop a register of individuals willing to undertake such work at short notice. To compile such a register would involve wide recruitment, with specific efforts to encourage black applicants for inclusion on the register, and non-racist assessment and interview procedures.

## University CE provision

Extramural provision continues to be a major responsibility for most CE departments. They generally offer a wide choice of courses to the general public in their area. This is not a real choice, however, if the information fails to reach you or if the programme fails to reflect your interests or the university locale and ethos are alienating. Black members of the public may not be taking advantage of extramural provision in representative numbers. Outreach and liaison work by department staff is time-consuming but invaluable in terms of making the provision known and developing courses in response to suggestions from minority communities. Publicity, courses in (and through) community languages, more black tutors, a more culturally diverse programme, inner-city venues and regular contact with community organizations in the patch are all conducive to attracting more black students.

Several university extramural departments do offer a relevant range of courses reflecting cultural diversity and antiracism. Birkbeck College, for instance, organizes student courses which mirror the diversity of socio-political and cultural experiences of different ethnic groups settled in London (Art from the Indian sub-continent, Palestinian Studies, the Jewish Experience, Latin American Studies, Problems of Democracy and Development in Africa, Modern African Music, Third World Cinema, Religious Studies). Liverpool's antiracist courses have included Race and Local Government, Race Issues in the 80s, Antiracist Education after Burnage, Black Vision (an exploration of black literature). Relevant antiracist, pluralist awareness training of all part-time tutors as part of their professional development would encourage the permeation of an antiracist and pluralist perspective into all courses on offer.

In some instances, courses explicitly about race and racism would benefit from school and post-school collaboration. Many schools, particularly in white areas, find that educational initiatives addressing the negative racial attitudes of pupils are undermined by parental prejudice. Relevant antiracist extramural courses for parents could be based at local schools which are simultaneously developing an antiracist approach with their pupils.

Many departments are developing certification within their liberal education programme, partly as an access route to higher education. At Warwick, for example, successful completion of an open entry certificated course provides entry to, and advanced standing on, a university part-time degree course. Such certificated courses should include studies of interest to minority ethnic groups and some could be vocationally oriented to develop the general academic skills relevant to a particular course of vocational training and to provide access to it. Birkbeck offers a certificate and diploma in Urban Community Studies, which is a modular course combining academic study with a vocational emphasis.

Many departments also provide certificates, diplomas and masters degrees in Continuing Education. Once again there is both the issue of attracting more black students and of the permeation of these courses with an antiracist perspective. Modular courses provide the opportunity to devote one or more units of study to racism and continuing education. The students on such courses, particularly at the masters level, are often senior people in their own field and have considerable power and influence. A race module that provides the opportunity for individuals to construct their own professional antiracist action plan thus makes the CE course a potential power house for antiracist educational change.

There is considerable evidence that black people are underrepresented in the professions and receive few professional training opportunities, despite Section 37 of the Race Relations Act, which allows special training exclusively for members of a particular racial group who are underrepresented in that specific field. With a growing number of CE departments becoming involved in continuing professional and vocational education (CPVE), this lack of black professionals is an issue that should be addressed by departments and discussed with the relevant professional bodies and employers. There is currently little work with black professionals, although Birmingham do provide a certificate in Pastoral Theology for pastors of black christian churches and the university is also responsible for a substantial programme of post-experience social work, which includes Cross-cultural Counselling, Cross-cultural Fostering and Adoption, Self-esteem and Identity in Black Children, Coping With Stress and Issues for Black Social Workers.

Sometimes, successful initiatives have crossed several categories of provision – liberal, vocational, access and professional. Goldsmiths' College, for example, have a media skills study course in their extramural programme which has a 100 per cent black intake and which combines media theory with practical options intended to prepare students for entry to higher education or employment in the media.

A department's research profile could also include work in the field of race and continuing education. It provides a fruitful field for participatory research through which departments can contribute to antiracist social change. Participatory research projects by students could focus on antiracist developments in their own institution – a local college of further education or teaching hospital – or on antiracist CE developments associated with the local authority or a community association. Research by the department's academic staff which is funded by the University Funding Council (UFC) might have a wider, national remit. A project to identify and remove institutional barriers associated with the lack of professional training opportunities mentioned above would be an example. The department's own antiracist developmental activity, both in-house and in the local community, could also be the object of some useful participatory research. Given the current lack of black academics and research students, there is good reason for collaboration with black organizations. Leicester

University's CE department has developed an initiative under the DES Innovation Scheme which is a joint project between the department and the Leicester Black Mental Health Group ('Ethnicity, Mental Health and Social Policy').

Education is often seen as potentially either a process of conserving the *status quo* or a tool for social change. Adult educators have traditionally allied themselves, if in rhetoric more than results, with the latter. The writings of Lovett describe initiatory and responsive models of education for the emancipation of the working class (Lovett 1990) and terms like 'empowerment' and 'liberating' are not uncommon. The idea of community education has been part of this 'radical orientation'. Although it is far from clear what work the word 'community' does, since it is often used to include everyone in a geographical location (the local community), or in far from homogeneous social groups (the Asian community), it does signal an alignment with the less privileged and powerful, the voiceless and dispossessed. 'Community centres' are usually based in materially deprived areas; they seek to be responsive to local needs and adopt an informal, participatory approach.

Continuing education departments are sympathetic to these movements and, more than many other university departments, have kept in touch with 'local communities' in developing collaborations and linkages of various kinds. 'Community'-based work with minority ethnic groups, sometimes undertaken in partnership with other inner-city providers, tends – although time-consuming and with little income-generating potential – to be seen as worthwhile.

## The question of resources

The University Funding Council has encouraged universities to bid for 'work with the disadvantaged'. Any work with minority ethnic groups which is able to count as such can attract the highest level of FTE payment. Entrepreneurial bids to various 'concerned' agencies can also raise money for 'inner-city' work, but this is often short-term funding. It is difficult to ensure that short-term projects get built into the infrastructure of institutions, although strategies to enable antiracist development to continue beyond the life of a short-term project can sometimes be devised during the funded period.

Grants provided to statutory and voluntary organizations for work connected with 'racial disadvantage' do tend to be short term in nature: injections of money to inner-city areas following urban unrest, for instance. Such funding is usually focused on meeting the 'needs' of black people as perceived by whites, rather than on either black needs as perceived by blacks or on dismantling white racism. To black people, it often seems that the main beneficiaries are the professionals (mainly white) involved in these funded projects.

The individuals who operate the funding agencies, whether these are charitable trusts, central government, local authorities or industry, share the racist assumptions of the wider society. Hence it may be easier for academics to obtain a research grant for a project which has its focus on 'minority groups' than for research which is directed at aspects of the racism of white institutions. Moreover, funding bodies, like other organizations, employ unwittingly discriminatory criteria – making bids with or by black groups particularly vulnerable. In an issue of *Voluntary Action*, Edgington comments on the underfunding of the black voluntary sector:

> The failure of central and local government mainstream funding programmes to respond to the requirements of black self help groups is now seen to be a major impediment to the long term development of effective black projects ... It is of course almost entirely predictable that a society which marginalises sections of its population and which excludes them from access to jobs, services and simple rules of justice should make funding inaccessible too.
>
> (Edgington 1981: 1)

Those charitable trusts whose specific remit relates to the promotion of racial equality have limited resources. They often have a local focus and a charitable function which excludes 'political' (but not education) action-oriented work. They are often restricted to funding registered charities (most black organizations are not so registered). For this reason, at the time I worked for AFFOR, a *multiracial* community organization in Birmingham which was registered as a charity, the Asian Resource Centre – a *black* self-help organization doing crucial inner-city welfare advice work – had to receive its funds from a well-disposed charitable trust, through the good offices of AFFOR.

University academics in continuing education should not be deterred from seeking funds for action-oriented antiracist work. However, we should seek to avoid pathologizing black people and recognize the importance of more black involvement in conceiving and implementing initiatives. (And, of course, much of our work does not require *additional* funding so much as a reorientation of current perspectives and practice.)

Financial support for HE students themselves is currently inadequate and there are various proposals to replace the grant system with student loans. Though some claim that this will enable more students to afford HE study, financial barriers will deter those in the lower socio-economic groups. The introduction of a loan system is likely to discourage many black and white working-class students for whom the shadow of debt will loom large.

## Warwick: A case study

In this section, I briefly describe the progress of antiracist education in the CE department of which I am a member, in order to provide a brief case study from which general insights may emerge. Decision making and development at Warwick University are based on an ethos and structure such that *departmental* identity is strong and influential. This encourages a measure of departmental competitiveness but it does not prevent considerable cooperation. Such cooperation may arise from the cross-disciplinary academic interests of individuals or from proposals that are in the common interest of more that one department. Much power, decision-making discretion, entrepreneurial opportunity and patronage are in the hands of 'strong departmental leaders' (Duke 1989). The CE department is an academic department, as any other, but it has an institution-wide brief: 'effectively to promote continuing education in the widest sense and in its many forms throughout the University, and in collaboration with other institutions and agencies in the region' (ibid.). It is a small but active department which includes in its activities: extramural provision for Warwickshire, Coventry and Solihull; access work in the region; the provision of part-time degree courses across the university; professional degree and postgraduate courses in continuing education; research, and national and international contributions to the practice and theory of lifelong learning.

At the moment, we have no black staff and have never had a full-time, permanent black academic staff member.[3] The Open Studies Programme includes some relevant provision, and professional courses offer a race module, but there is no permeation of an antiracist pluralist perspective across the curriculum. We have developed links and collaborative ventures with organizations and individuals in Coventry's inner-city and are supporting the establishment of the university's new education centre in Hillfields, a 'deprived' area of the city. (This is a promising venture, and has attracted a good, small multiracial staff.)

Our response to the UCACE and follow-up surveys shows us to be at least average in our antiracist development, and typical in that, like most CE departments, there have been small-scale initiatives arising from the interests of individual academics and some special and general relevant provision, but without structural or curriculum permeation across the department as a whole. The department does not have a written antiracist or equal opportunities policy statement, though equal opportunities feature in its recently adopted Mission Statement. Although the job description for my own post indicated the desirability of an interest in, and experience of, work with minority ethnic groups, a reference to 'equal opportunity' related experience is not a standard part of all job descriptions. We do not advertise in the minority ethnic group press, although we have decided to set up a register of interested individuals to fill part-time or fractional posts quickly and without patronage. This decision is taking a considerable time to implement. We do not shortlist according to anti-racist criteria. We do include equal opportunities questions when interviewing for new full-time academic posts, but not for part-time Open Studies tutors. Although the question of equal opportunities is raised in academic interviews, the candidate's ability to demonstrate relevant interests and experience is not one of the specific and definite requirements for obtaining the post. It thus becomes asked as a fairly tokenistic gesture – a matter of form and ritual rather than as a real expression of the will to build up a committed team. Neither the academic or support staff have received antiracist training as part of a collective staff development. There are very few black students coming into the department or university through the various access routes. We do not monitor the ethnic background of our students or the development of antiracist practices in our work.

This general picture shows some positive development but, given the commitment of several individuals and the entrepreneurial climate, less than one might expect. We see some good practice arising from individual initiatives but antiracism has not become part of the fabric and functioning of departmental routine. A similar picture emerges if we consider other aspects of equal opportunities. Thus, the Open Studies co-ordinator has established some gender and some special needs provision, e.g. a 'Women into Science' certificate. The support staff are developing ideas about the department taking some initiative in relation to their own continuing professional development. Again we see individual initiative but not, yet, real structural change. The questions to be asked are: what factors have inhibited greater progress, what has facilitated the progress to date and how could more be achieved?

At one level, it is tempting to say that this limited progress is due to the pressure on time, energy and resources. Several colleagues did say this when interviewed and it contains much validity. However, this pressure on time is precisely why antiracist change cannot be left to the goodwill and initiative of individuals. The collective, if committed, must find ways of institutionalizing antiracist practice so that it is built into the organizational structures and routine processes in each area of the department's work. This should include building antiracist and other equal opportunities criteria into the assessment of quality of provision and antiracist achievement into the appraisal of individual academics.

Paradoxically, the strong leadership model at Warwick is both conducive to antiracist progress and inhibiting of it. A well-intentioned departmental leader encourages development at the level of individual initiative but strong leadership becomes self-defeating beyond this limited point, which the more progressive departments have now reached. Democratic development is not best achieved through centralized and concentrated power and patronage, but through genuinely shared and devolved decision making. Radical change comes from democratic processes and structures rather than from strong leaders or charismatic individuals. Such democratic decisions take longer to achieve than do the rapid decisions of one person. Thus the rate of change may appear to slow down when more fundamental movements begin to take place. In any university, the culture of individual autonomy and achievement may simultaneously encourage (to a limited degree) and inhibit (at a more fundamental level) the progress of co-operative democratization.

What would help to shift progress from the level of individual initiative to the development of structural level change? In staffing the department, all job descriptions could refer to interest and experience in aspects of equal opportunities and such experience could be an explicit requirement built into shortlisting and interview criteria. As one aspect of this, departments could explicitly acknowledge the value of recruiting black academic staff and of building a team which represents a variety of cultural backgrounds. Collective staff development through equal opportunities training would help to establish a pluralist and antiracist perspective across the curriculum. Such training should also be offered to support staff who, in being part of CE provision, often have a key role in the department's relations with its clients. Access initiatives should directly address race issues and the recruitment of black students. Failing this, access developments which are otherwise progressive will fail proportionately to include black people. Similarly, new projects with inreach (mainstreaming) or outreach (community) dimensions should have an antiracist aspect built into their aims and objectives.

A department wishing to achieve this degree of permeation may need to set up a working group to monitor developments and to draw up an action plan with time-scaled targets. Such an action plan might include the construction of a written policy to guide staffing and training objectives and resource allocation. Without this kind of specific and collective attention to race issues, an entrepreneurial ethos will not necessarily produce antiracist *outcomes*: well-intentioned rhetoric will not lead to change and black people will not benefit from 'equity' projects. Warwick University has been described as a 'selfish and therefore a successful and relatively accessible institution' (Duke 1989). But the question remains – successful and accessible for whom?

# 5 | Change Agents and Models: A UCACE Survey Revisited

In 1988, the University Council for Adult and Continuing Education (UCACE) established a working party to analyse existing provision by university continuing education for the minority ethnic communities. It was also to make recommendations for new initiatives and for the removal of barriers to access. The working party undertook a survey of 40 university departments and, believing that departments could learn much from each other, they provided departmental details of the varied forms of innovative work which they found (UCACE 1990). I have referred already to some of that current departmental work as illustrative of good practice. The UCACE report also provides some guidance on improving practice and provision, plus thirteen recommendations (see Appendix 2). Some of these recommendations cover curriculum and institutional development and others reflect an assumption that CE departments can be catalysts for antiracist mainstream development across their universities.

Having been a member of the UCACE Working Group, I subsequently decided to discover what action university CE departments had taken to implement the UCACE recommendations to improve their own provisions and to influence their universities as a whole. In a sense, these actions provide examples of CE departments as models of (partial) antiracist continuing education and as antiracist change agents seeking to influence their universities.

Written responses to a letter of enquiry indicated that by October 1990 two-thirds of departments had undertaken new initiatives *since* the UCACE survey was completed and just over one-third had undertaken initiatives at *both* the department and university levels (Leicester and Lovell 1991). New special provision has been developed in six categories (certified extra-mural courses; access; community education, outreach provision, diploma and MEd; action research; and general programme provision), some with a pluralist and some with an antiracist dimension. New anti-discriminatory procedures for the recruitment of students, such as advertising in the local ethnic minority group press, have also been initiated and the point was made that attracting black students tends to increase each year as past and present black students pass on information through their own networks. Staff recruitment and professional development initiatives were also reported, while across the university progress has been made in heightening awareness in relation to the admission of black students and academic staff development. There was, however, little on professional and vocational courses or the development of monitoring procedures for reviewing and assessing the departments' progress in antiracist initiatives. In what follows, I highlight points of insight and examples of good practice, indicating strategies and developments from which we can learn.

The inquiry went to heads of departments, some of whom answered it themselves, some circulated it round their department for comment and some passed it to a particular member of staff. The responses often name individuals responsible for, or doing, relevant work. The general picture is one of committed individuals taking initiatives rather than of departmental policy in action across the departments. This is not to say that departments are unaware of the desirability of a departmental response and some are clearly moving in that direction:

> After departmental reorganization, the department is now ready to tackle equal opportunities at a departmental level (rather than as a number of individual initiatives). Our recent departmental submission to the university identifies equal opportunities as an important area where we need to take concerted action as providers.
>
> (Southampton)

Almost all responses indicate at least implicit, and often explicit, agreement with equal opportunities and antiracism:

> In my own department, there is a strong realization of the need to promote equal opportunities and to counter racism wherever it is found.
>
> (Durham)

Only one response had a different view, exhibiting what Halstead categorized as 'colour blind racism':

> This is a very small department, and for that reason we do not have any specific provision of the type in which you are interested. However, the policy of the department and of the university is to make no distinctions between students on ethnic grounds, and I am satisfied that this policy is implemented.

There is widely shared regret that more has not been achieved, but there is optimism about future plans and developments, tempered by the recognition of difficulties (particularly staffing constraints) with small, or changing, and usually ethnically homogeneous staff facing a variety of pressures and demands:

> Some time ago we began to establish links with ethnic minority groups and teachers in Southampton. This involved a number of small-scale education and training initiatives as well as an (unsuccessful) attempt to launch a Return To Study course specifically geared to the black community. Since then, some links have been maintained but staff changes and departmental reorganization have made it difficult to build actively on the initial work. Present developments are restricted by having an all-white full-time staff group.
>
> (Southampton)

It was striking that almost all the responses (some implicitly, and some explicitly) shared the UCACE assumption that influencing the university as a whole is an appropriate objective for CE departments to adopt, and in some universities this is an official role:

> Because the new Board will have a watching brief for all continuing education within the university, unlike the current Board of Extra-Mural Studies, it will be able to influence policy and practice in this area.
>
> (Cambridge)

The opposite, minority view was stated thus:

> Certainly, I personally would not try to persuade other departments to develop this (or any other provision); the detailed course curriculum for each department is the responsibility of that department (subject to the overall authority of their Faculty Board and Senate).

Another response pointed up the prior need for departments to heighten their own awareness and knowledge, and this seems to me to be an obvious but important point:

> Yes, departments such as ours must lead the way within the university but not from either a naive/benevolent or shrill standpoint. We can only lead effectively from a critically informed perspective.
>
> (Nottingham)

One department implicitly made a distinction between a general lead role in antiracism, which was felt to be inappropriate, and collaboration with the university in areas relevant to continuing education, such as staff development:

I think the role of my department would be to engage with the Staff Development personnel to think of ways of disseminating an awareness of equal opportunities and antiracist issues. Towards this end, I shall bring forward your paper to our Board of Studies, and hope that from that can arise some clear recommendation for our Staff Development personnel with a view to working closely with them to deal with such issues throughout the university.

(Durham)

Collaboration with others in the university was one of the general strategies which the responses indicate that departments have used in attempts to influence university-wide developments. Other striking instances of collaborative initiatives include:

1. Individual members of departments cooperating with other university staff as part of the university's equal opportunities committee, or equal opportunity policy working group.
2. Department co-ordination of an initiative to collaborate with other interested departments to present a paper to the relevant university committees on the implications of extending the equal opportunities policy to cover the entire university community.
3. Joint initiatives between the department and the university's associated colleges of higher education to heighten awareness of antiracist policies and practices and to improve provision and support for black students at the pre-higher and higher education stages.
4. Collaboration with the university admissions committee. Good practice associated with this initiative at Lancaster was the inclusion of *planned outcomes* of the collaboration, including:

   • revised, targeted admission procedures (but not different entry qualifications);
   • a limited experiment with individual students offering non-standard entry qualifications;
   • input into the academic staff development programme.

5. Collaboration with other parts of the university (students' union, counselling service, academic registrar, staff development section) to run a two-day induction course for mature entrants to the university. Again, in addition to the good practice of collaboration with relevant others, this initiative incorporated plans to monitor the progress and problems of these mature entrants and to feed the results back into the university staff development process.
6. Collaboration with other university staff and a variety of outside providers, including some Section 11 workers, on an access conference

introduced by the vice-chancellor. The first half of the conference was designed so that staff would collectively identify and investigate barriers to access faced by mature students in relation to the university as a whole. This focused very much on equal opportunities issues. Recommendations from the conference have gone to other relevant committees of the university and the department is setting up an access board of study with representation from mature students, outside providers and internal departments.

There are several good features in this instance of collaborative activity. The CE department is making use of its greater links outside the university to bring the institution into contact with outside providers; the problems of access are to be identified across the university; the vice-chancellor's seal of approval is secured; recommendations go on to university committees to ensure further action and change; and the access board of study will have three-fold representation.

Another general strategy adopted by departments was to use departmental influence:

• through representation on university committees to influence those committees, e.g. the committee for the training of university teachers;
• through accepting the role of equal opportunities co-ordinator for the faculty of educational studies and thereby influencing developments at the faculty and university levels;
• through developing the equal opportunities dimensions of any papers to be written for, and presented to, a university committee.

Gratifyingly, much use was made of the UCACE report and recommendations, within departments and across the university, to get antiracist issues on to various agendas and in some cases to stimulate a review of current practice or of antiracist progress. This third strategy is a useful one in relation to other reports and recommendations about race relations, ethnic diversity, multiculturalism, antiracism, equal opportunities and so on. These appear at fairly regular intervals from bodies like, for instance, the Commission for Racial Equality and professional organizations. Particularly useful are those that emanate from bodies which carry clout for academics. Progressive instances of these should always be tabled for discussion and action. For example, the Committee of Vice-Chancellors and Principals (CVCP 1991) has relatively recently issued a useful report on equal opportunities. This recommends appropriate action in relation to the employment of black people, women and people with disabilities. It recommends taking advantage of those sections of the Sex Discrimination Act 1975 and the Race Relations Act 1976 which allow for positive action. It includes guidance on employment practice, the formulation, implementation and monitoring of the institution's equal opportunities policy, training and statistical record-keeping.

One department's response concentrated on the issue of permeation. They use a 'Freirean philosophy', keep up with the antiracist literature, encourage an on-going critical stance to staff and student assumptions ('continually examine our own thought and action with reference to all sorts of oppression') and ensure that students 'understand not only the historical roots of racism but the global relations which perpetuate it'.

Aberystwyth provides special courses which introduce newcomers of all backgrounds to the history, literature and culture of Wales, including the teaching of the Welsh language. They also run a two-month course in Third World Development Studies for students from India and Africa, who have an advisory role in their home country. Although these are not black British students, one of the spin-offs has been to raise collegiate awareness of the needs of minority ethnic communities – though in an area where they total very small numbers in the college's actual hinterland.

Just as there were several examples of inreach into the university, the responses provided instances of good outreach work. One university attempts to link their black students with African-Caribbean and Asian fieldwork supervisors from the local community. Another is conducting 'market research' among local Asian communities and developing outreach provision based on it, while bidding to the UFC for development money for this work. Negotiating the Curriculum with Unwaged Adults, an action-research project funded by the Further Education Unit (FEU), focused on the black community and made some progress in identifying an appropriate antiracist curriculum in relation to 'enterprise' development. The same university (Southampton) provided an example of outreach collaboration where the department, the regional Replan office, and the local Community Relations Council worked together to secure a Punjabi script typewriter and located it at an inner-city adult education centre.

While much of the work described in this section would have taken place without the UCACE recommendations, it is pleasing that many departments did make good use of the report, particularly since the use of it made by UCACE itself was at first disappointing: amounting to a low-key infusion into the 1991 annual conference and an unsuccessful bid to UFC for a development officer to work with departments on the recommendations. UCACE was unable to subsidize travel to the conference for working group members who required it; as a result, none of the group's black members were present. Moreover, because discussion of the report became one strand in an option session, not everyone who attended was able to benefit from that discussion. Nor was the report on the agenda of the UCACE council meeting that took place at the end of the conference: it was only discussed there (briefly) at the request of a council member.

There are general lessons to be learned for working groups set up by UCACE and similar bodies.[1] Such groups usually represent considerable collective experience, bringing together hard-working and committed individuals. It is therefore advisable for groups of this kind (particularly those working on equal opportunities issues) to reach some agreements with the commissioning body at the outset – not just over their terms of reference but also on how the work of the group will be disseminated and made use of and about resources and strategies for the implementation of such recommendations as may emerge.

**Part 2**
Continuing Antiracist
Education: The University
Transformed

# 6 | Coming of Age: The Mature University

## The idea of higher education

'Primary education' suggests the initial stages of education: prime in coming first and laying foundations. 'Secondary' indicates a second stage of building on those foundations. 'Further education' is a continuation of this schooling. Since 'further' suggests a continuation of schooling, 'higher education' would seem not just to refer to another chronological stage. Higher education, while it may (even necessarily) come later than the education offered during schooling, is in some other way distinct from it too. There must be a sense in which the education offered is inherently 'higher' as well as chronologically later. What, then, is distinctive about 'higher education' that makes it somehow 'higher' than the other stages – primary, secondary and further?

I would suggest that higher education is characterized by being a 'second-order' activity; that is to say, it is a meta-activity focused on the first-order material provided by earlier stages of education. It operates over and above such material and is higher in *that* sense. Given my emphasis on education as the pursuit of worthwhile knowledge, I would see higher education as the final – although unending – stage in the pursuit of knowledge. At this stage, the individual develops analytical skills and thereby a much broader understanding of our collective knowledge, and may even add to it. Second-order critical analysis of what is already known generates new knowledge in both these senses: it develops individual understanding at this second-order level and is part of the process by which our collective forms of knowledge are further developed and may be transformed.

Ronald Barnett (1990), in *The Idea of Higher Education*, similarly argues that there is a conceptual difference between primary and higher education which is not simply a matter of the ages of those undergoing the associated educational processes – although the students' maturity may justifiably affect the control they might enjoy over the direction, pacing, evaluation and assessment of their own learning. Like me, he sees the conceptual difference in terms of higher-order understanding:

> The central claim made here is that 'higher education' is essentially a matter of the development of the mind of the individual student. It is not just any kind of development that the idea points to. An educational process can be termed higher education when the student is carried on to levels of reasoning which make possible critical reflection on his or her experiences, whether consisting of propositional knowledge or of knowledge through action. These levels of reasoning and reflection are 'higher' because they enable the student to take a view (from above, as it were) of what has been learned. Simply, 'higher education' resides in the higher-order states of mind.
>
> (Barnett 1990: 202)

It is a common and mistaken assumption that such higher-order states of mind can only be attained by a clever and elite few. The positive connotation of 'higher' then becomes linked to, and reinforces, a hierarchical and elitist attitude to those who can and have benefited compared to those who supposedly cannot. That certain groups are disproportionately underrepresented in higher education is one indication that discriminatory social processes rather than ceilings of innate ability determine entry into higher education. Many more individuals could benefit from higher education if we were to continue to move towards a mass rather than an elitist system. A mass system that catered for all who could benefit, and which was such that many more would wish to do so, would be much more representative of the general population and thus more racially and culturally diverse.

The acquisition of worthwhile knowledge develops the inherently valuable higher-order states of mind to which I have referred and, thus, education is intrinsically valuable and not to be prized solely for instrumental purposes. Vocational education must be more than mere training, for example (Hirst and Peters 1970). This is not to deny that it may also have instrumental value. Although a liberal education is concerned with the intrinsically worthwhile, a logically necessary consequence is that we are providing knowledge and understanding that have the most general relevance and utility for anything one is likely to want to do (Bailey 1984).

Barnett (1990) believes that liberal education is threatened by a double epistemological and sociological undermining. The epistemological undermining is due to 'modern philosophical and theoretical developments' – the kind of constructivist epistemology espoused in this book. The sociological undermining comes from the pressure of social interests on the institution. Much of Barnett's book is relevant to, and compatible with, the epistemological presuppositions of my own arguments and not dissimilar to what I shall argue about knowledge and research. But there is a significant difference. Barnett sees research as not inherently part of the conception of higher education; for him, the teaching process is paramount and central. However, because of the way that (ironically) we both conceive the nature of knowledge, I would argue that teaching and learning at this higher level contributes to the construction of objective knowledge, and thus is an aspect of 'research'. Teaching and research are both key and interrelated aspects of higher education, conceived as a second-order stage of the pursuit of worthwhile knowledge.

## The mature university

I have suggested that through inreach and outreach activity, CE departments can and are acting as change agents. By increasing, for mature students, both access to their institution and its suitability to receive them, activist departments are in the process of changing the nature of the universities. As yet, these access and accessibility aims have only partly been realized, but continuing education is gaining ground.

However, as will be clear in the forthcoming discussions about access courses and admission procedures, progressive change may fail black communities while yet serving other socially and economically 'disadvantaged' groups. The strategies devised and the actions taken to mainstream continuing education must be such that the outcomes achieved are anti-racist, as well as desirable according to other progressive and equity-based criteria – changes that include introducing access courses, accreditation of prior experiential learning (APEL), credit accumulation and transfer (CATS), modularization, developing part-time degrees and open college networks (OCN), outreach provision, and so on.

In this section, I will explore why such current movements in higher education are associated with continuing education, and seek to show in what their coherence consists.

In his recent book in this series, Chris Duke has argued that we are in the process of making a paradigm shift from conceptualizing the university in the old, elitist, traditional way to seeing it as a lifelong resource centre (Duke 1992). The Khunian notion of paradigm and paradigm shifts is helpful in this context. Kuhn distinguishes between two senses or 'paradigm' which are blended in his ideas about scientific revolutions: paradigm as 'disciplinary matrix' and paradigm as 'achieved result'. The 'disciplinary matrix' is the patterns of education and communication by which a particular scientific community share an inextricably combined mixture of theory, methods and standards. Paradigm as 'achieved result' refers to the body of achievement coming out of the disciplinary matrix. Applying this to continuing education, one would say that continuing educators share an interlinked package of theory, methods and standards through which they conceive and practise their disciplinary field, and that this is currently generating changes (achieved results) in higher education. One could claim that this shared disciplinary matrix is gaining wider currency in the universities, beyond the CE departments, and that there are signs that the rate of such change is increasing to the point (though this is debatable) of HE revolution.[1] Evidence for the first claim has been drawn, for example, from the university planning statements and offers submitted to the University Funding Council (UFC) in June 1990 (Duke 1992). Evidence for the second claim could be seen in the way that the 1980s rhetoric on widening access has gained momentum; so that in the early 1990s there has been a rapid growth of support and promotion of access, through open college networks, and more active collaboration between further and higher education institutions.

The inextricable mixture of 'theories, methods and standards' shared by adult educators include as key elements: a theory of education that is based on notions of lifelong learning for all, and which incorporates an equity-grounded belief that higher education should be available to all who want it and could benefit from it; and theories about the nature, needs and interests of mature students as relevant to HE provision. These theories have implications for institutional ethos, organization and curriculum and have achieved valuable teaching and research methodologies. They also presuppose standards of flexibility (of provision), plurality (of provision, curriculum and clientele), student-centredness of approach, with justice as an overarching value.

This adult educators' 'intellectual matrix' generates practices to promote lifelong learning. In other words, it encourages practices that would permit access to higher education at all stages of the adult life cycle and that would constitute an institutional organization and ethos appropriate to mature students. Thus a conception of lifelong learning provides a framework of aims which determines the changes to be sought and which gives relevant contemporary movements in higher education their coherence (see Fig. 1). We could call this framework and the practices it supports, *the paradigm of the mature university.*

In my view, we are in a period of flux between the traditional and currently dominant model of the university and at least two other discernible paradigms (see Table 1). The differences between these will be made clearer in the following chapters. All three will continue to be a part (to different degrees in different institutions) of higher education

**Figure 1**  Lifelong learning and racist/antiracist versions

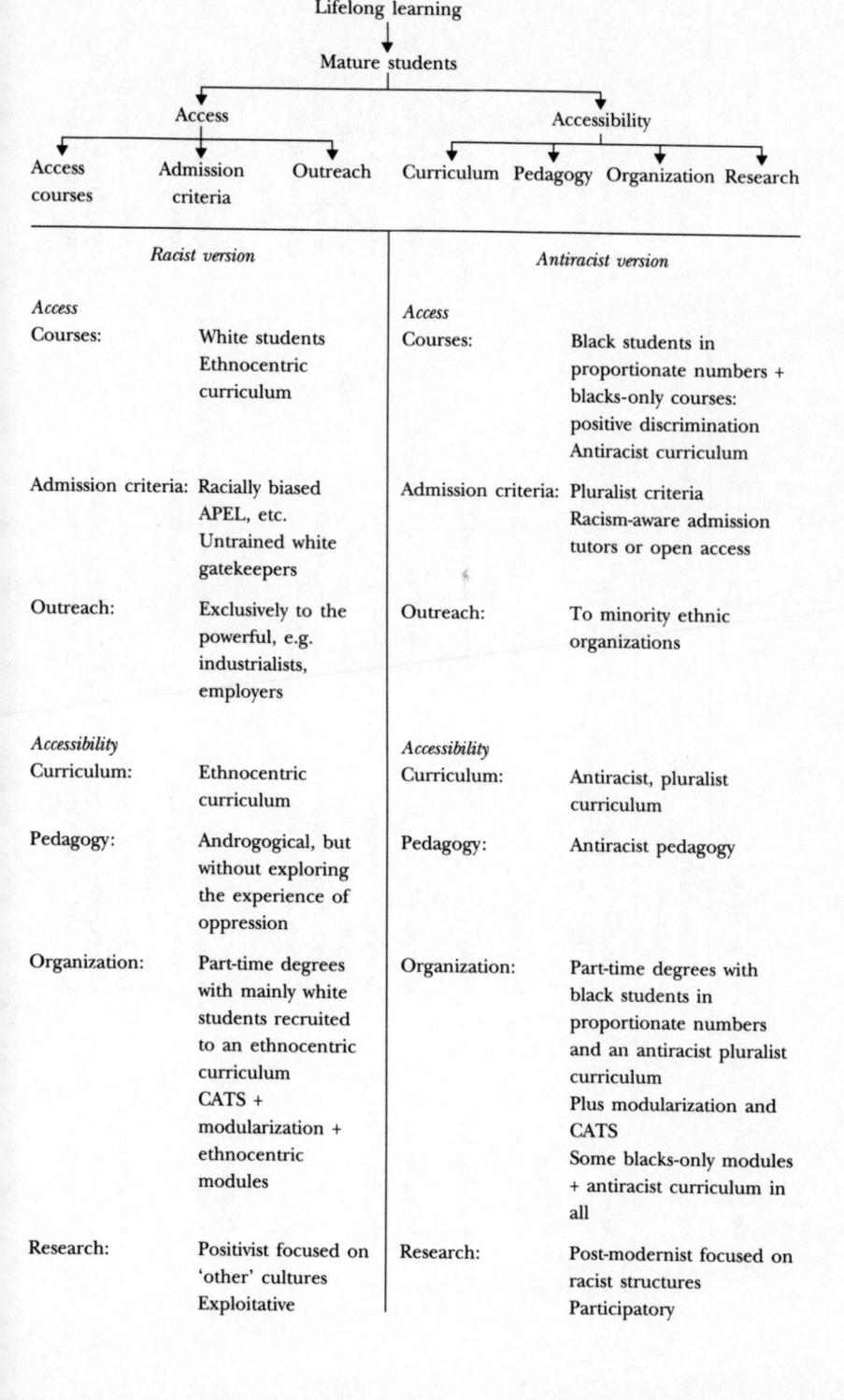

| Racist version | | Antiracist version | |
|---|---|---|---|
| *Access* | | *Access* | |
| Courses: | White students Ethnocentric curriculum | Courses: | Black students in proportionate numbers + blacks-only courses: positive discrimination Antiracist curriculum |
| Admission criteria: | Racially biased APEL, etc. Untrained white gatekeepers | Admission criteria: | Pluralist criteria Racism-aware admission tutors or open access |
| Outreach: | Exclusively to the powerful, e.g. industrialists, employers | Outreach: | To minority ethnic organizations |
| *Accessibility* | | *Accessibility* | |
| Curriculum: | Ethnocentric curriculum | Curriculum: | Antiracist, pluralist curriculum |
| Pedagogy: | Androgogical, but without exploring the experience of oppression | Pedagogy: | Antiracist pedagogy |
| Organization: | Part-time degrees with mainly white students recruited to an ethnocentric curriculum CATS + modularization + ethnocentric modules | Organization: | Part-time degrees with black students in proportionate numbers and an antiracist pluralist curriculum Plus modularization and CATS Some blacks-only modules + antiracist curriculum in all |
| Research: | Positivist focused on 'other' cultures Exploitative | Research: | Post-modernist focused on racist structures Participatory |

**Table 1** Three paradigms of the university

| | The ivory tower or traditional university | The university of market forces | The mature university |
|---|---|---|---|
| 1. Theory | Education produces 'The Educated Man' | Education for pragmatic ends | Education facilitates lifelong learning |
| 2. Methods | | | |
| • Teaching | Lectures | Most cost-effective in a given situation | Discussion-based |
| • Research | Positivistic | Driven by market forces | Action-oriented and participatory |
| 3. Standards/values | | | |
| • Organization | Discipline-based | Controlled and managed | Flexible, student-centred |
| | Academic excellence Pursuit of (monolithic) disciplinary knowledge Rigour and authority | Efficiency Knowledge for utilitarian ends and empirical control Utility | Equality with quality Interdisciplinary and pluralistic knowledge Flexibility and cultural synthesis |
| 4. Practices | | | |
| • Admission | Identify a stream of excellence through competitive entry | Marketing of competing courses for competing students | Open, non-competitive entry |
| • Curriculum | Discipline-based curriculum Liberal education | Vocational curriculum Enterprise education | Interdisciplinary curriculum Empowerment education |
| • Outcomes | Qualified social elite | Thatcherite citizens | Democratic citizens |

5. Associated discourse

| Selection | Marketing | Access |
|---|---|---|
| A levels | Demand | Non-traditional entry, open entry |
| Disciplines (mastery) | Competence | Learning |
| Lectures | Cost-effective teaching | Experiential learning |
| Academic | Enterprise | Empowerment |
| Grants | Loans | Student support |
| Educated | Employable | Developing |
| Class of degree | Vocational qualifications | Meaning perspective, conscientization |
| Appraisal | Audit | Self-assessment |
| Guide | Control | Facilitate |
| Centre of excellence | Cost centre | Community |
| Academic standing | Validation | Partnership |

guiding assumptions and practices. Some aspects of one paradigm may be compatible with, or even shared by, another. For example, traditional conceptions of a liberal education partly overlap with the concept of life-long learning (Leicester 1989a). Other aspects are in tension, e.g. ideals of competition and of access. Yet others may be in direct conflict, such as responding to market forces on the one hand or to social welfare on the other.

The practices generated by the paradigm of the mature university include some that do not match well with current HE provision in the traditional mode, and may be contested. When paradigms clash, since standards of rationality are internal to each, choice between them is more a matter of negotiation, dialogue and persuasion than of producing an irrefutable argument convincing to all (Leicester 1992).

It is useful to distinguish between these three paradigms because, in being clear about the paradigm of the mature university, as continuing educators we can be more single-minded in its service – seeking to maximize its influence and predominance in situations of conflict with either or both of the other two paradigms.

## Growing up

How can the traditional university, in these market-driven times, grow into the mature institution? Again the notion of a paradigm shift is useful. Because intellectual matrix and achieved results are interlinked, which comes first is a chicken and egg question. Change agents must therefore work on both levels. Achieving relevant practices influences the perceptions of colleagues beyond the department, who begin to understand the new intellectual matrix. Conversely, increased understanding engenders a greater readiness to accept existing, and yet more, CE initiatives (achieved results), with value-backed persuasion as the appropriate approach. Converting influential individuals – heads of department, admissions tutors, etc. – is crucial if traditional conservatism is not to prevent or subvert such initiatives.

The pervasive influence of the market forces paradigm must also be used rather than ignored. For example, the emphasis placed by the Jarratt Committee (1985) on efficiency and management is part of that influence. Universities are required, as a condition of receiving extra funds, to reserve monies for incentive (merit) salary increments, and to appraise all academic staff using UFC-approved appraisal schemes. Within the university, meritorious work that benefits 'socially deprived' groups (including minority ethnic groups) *could* be recognized for such salary increments and an antiracist dimension built into staff appraisal. If academic staff were aware that such work carries significant brownie points towards merit awards (and promotion) and that lack of attention to equal opportunities aspects of their research, teaching and administration will be noted during the appraisal process, then both the carrot-and-stick approaches to institutional change will have been used effectively in two crucial parts of the system.

Parry points to a useful National Advisory Body (NAB) suggestion that is also in this opportunistic mode of inserting or securing equal opportunities dimensions into potentially 'market'-driven developments.

> The principle of targeting, collaboration and progression underpinning access programmes in further education and access contracts in secondary education are likely to figure large in the transition to a more open and plural system of higher education, but the persistence of severe skill shortages may see these principles increasingly deployed in programmes to meet manpower requirements rather than equal opportunity objectives. However, if government and funding bodies in higher education have to return to selective initiatives to promote recruitment or development in particular fields there may be another opportunity to recommend that targets for under represented groups as well as for subject areas be built into contractual agreements with higher education institutions (NAB 1988).

As Figure 1 indicates, at any point, progressive CE initiatives may fail to be antiracist. For example, increasing and supporting access courses should include attention to the recruitment of black students. In different regions, this might be most effectively done through blacks-only courses or through targeted recruitment to increase the proportion of black students. A positive experience of the access course by the initial black student population will help subsequent recruitment – as word-of-mouth recommendations feed into black networks. If some of the access course staff are black, this is likely to facilitate a positive experience and evaluation of the course. Similar points could be made in relation to the development of other provisions for mature students, e.g. part-time degrees, or the transformation of courses into a modular structure. The positive experience of teaching a multiracial group will, in turn, encourage lecturers to support initiatives to recruit a diverse student body.

In order to attain an *antiracist* mature university, it is necessary to be clear about what that means in relation to *all* aspects of university life – access, research, teaching, curriculum and university organization. By understanding what these would be like if transformed by antiracism, we would know what to aim for. As is encapsulated in Figure 1, 'the mature university' is both about access for mature students and also about internal suitability (accessibility) to their needs. In what follows, access and accessibility (in terms of research, teaching, curriculum and university organization) will be discussed. What would these be like, in an antiracist environment, within the mature university?

# 7 | Outreach: Antiracist Access

## The access movement

The access movement has rapidly expanded over the past decade. Encouraged by government support, which is motivated by pragmatic considerations concerning the declining number of 18-year-olds in the population and the need for a more highly educated workforce, it was given impetus by the jolt to local authorities from the inner-city uprisings of the early 1980s and fuelled by the ideological commitment of adult education to 'equal opportunities' (Brennan 1989).

Many influential official bodies have added their voices to the 1980s emphasis on the importance of increasing access to higher education, including the professional associations of teachers in further and higher education, the National Advisory Body (NAB), the Council for National Academic Awards (CNAA), the Standing Conference on University Entrance, the Training Agency, the Council for Engineering, the Foundation for Science and Technology and the Royal Society of Arts (Parry and Wake 1990). Official sanction of access courses will have limited impact on economically deprived groups, however, if it is unaccompanied by financial support. Local government has been more generous than central government in providing financial incentives (Wagner 1989). Whatever new forms of government support emerge from current discussions, their impact on socially and economically disadvantaged groups will be a crucial factor for the participation of black students in higher education.

Currently, in addition to disproportionately few black staff, there are also disproportionately few black students in higher education – disproportionate, that is, to their numbers in the general population. Exact proportions of black applicants are not known. Although the University Central Council on Admissions (UCCA) and the Polytechnics Central Admissions System (PCAS) agreed to include an ethnicity question on application forms for the 1990 cohort, the information was not passed on to admissions tutors because of concern – particularly by the Committee of Vice-Chancellors and Principals (CVCP) – about positive discrimination. More recently, and following a report from the University of Warwick Centre for Ethnic Relations (Taylor 1992), the CVCP has reversed this decision. The report confirms that acceptance rates vary significantly between ethnic groups, even when factors such as students' qualifications and social class are taken into account. Admission tutors are therefore now to receive the information about ethnicity *and* CVCP guidance to ensure that black applicants are not penalized.

Seeking to open the university to 'non-traditional' students is a tradition of university adult education, which rejects the current model of the university as an 'expensive finishing school' (Duke 1988: 12) for the 18-year-old sons and daughters of the professional classes. As well as running extramural and other open entry courses, CE departments are part of the current movement to develop a variety of admissions procedures and access courses which will facilitate access to the mainstream of the university by economically disadvantaged groups. Unfortunately, these progressive devices are still not benefiting black students in proportionate numbers.

## 'Big A' and 'little a' access

A useful distinction is often made between two strands in the access movement: first, devices such as the development of access courses and of more flexible admissions procedures, which facilitate *entry* into the university by black and other currently excluded groups ('big A' access); and, second, the recognition of the need to make the institution, in its curriculum and ethos, more responsive to their presence and conducive to its continuation and growth ('little a' access) (Fulton 1989). There is some debate about how much increasing that presence through 'big A' access will *itself* lead to the requisite institutional change. Many adult educators who are active in creating more flexible and fairer entry structures as the most immediate and achievable step towards equity, may also believe that the institution should and could change in anti-oppressive ways and that *additional* strategies will be required to achieve this change.

In the literature on equal opportunities in education, a distinction has been made between the liberal and radical approaches. The liberal approach is to promote equal opportunities for each individual irrespective of race, class, gender, disability, etc. The aim is to enable individuals to compete for goods on an equal basis and entails removing barriers based on race. The radical approach is to promote equal opportunities for disadvantaged social groups. The aim is to ensure that goods are distributed such that these groups are proportionately advantaged. In the context of 'big A' access to higher education (taken to be a social good), the liberal approach construes A level entry to higher education at eighteen as unfair to mature individuals who may have experienced at school unfair racist barriers to formal educational achievement. This justifies the provision of access courses and the constructing of alternative admissions criteria such as the accreditation of prior experiential learning (APEL). The current movement to standardize access courses clearly springs from this ideology. The access course becomes an alternative route to higher education – a route still based on crossing a boundary by reaching a standard, but having fewer race-, gender- or class-based hurdles along the way. The more radical approach, which could be seen as social engineering, advocates positive discrimination within this process (in recruitment, perhaps, or in weighting assessment) to enable proportionate numbers from disadvantaged groups to gain entry into higher education.

In the second, broader sense of 'little a' access, the focus is on institutional change. There is a belief that the HE curriculum will change *because* of these new clients. The current curriculum has a white, male, middle-class orientation. The assumption is that the presence of the new constituencies will encourage women's studies and issues, cultural pluralism and a diversity of perspectives, and that more mature students, coming from student-centred, negotiated, interdisciplinary access courses, will influence the curriculum and pedagogy of the receiving institutions. Such beliefs presumably include a normative element too: that these *should* change in this responsive manner. (Again, one could distinguish between a liberal and a radical approach to such institutional change.)

## Scaling the Ivory Tower

Having outlined these broad questions concerned with the distinction between the two senses of access (entry and accessibility), I turn now to the former, and the more specific issue of 'big A' access courses and admissions criteria.

Although there are some 500 access courses across 96 LEAs, open access programmes have tended to attract small numbers of black students unless real efforts have been made to reach black communities. On the whole, polytechnics have made more of an effort and have shown what effective access policies can achieve. For example, in 1988, 30 per cent of the graduates of the Polytechnic of North London were from minority ethnic groups. There are issues, then, about the recruitment and admissions procedures of access courses themselves: Do they embody antiracist recruitment practice? Is the curriculum antiracist? Are some of the access tutors black?

Predominantly white courses (access or mainstream higher education) may present problems of isolation and even alienation for their few black students:

> On the one hand, such is conventional wisdom and popular stereo-type, they are expected to find more difficulties in their studies than other students. On the other hand, their tutors, inexperienced in handling racial and ethnic issues, turn to them for advice and assistance. This combination of low academic expectation and high demand for personal involvement and contribution is a significant burden, but rarely recognised as such.
>
> (UCACE 1990: 8)

Some access courses are specifically targeted at minority ethnic groups. The term 'targeting', commonly used in this context, with its aggressive shooting associations, echoes for me the earlier discussion about why and for whose benefit non-traditional students are sought. If it is in order to meet the pragmatic needs of an institution which will itself remain un-changed, could a half-conscious recognition of this account for relatively low take up?

Where courses are for black people only, students can share their ex-perience of being black in Britain and offer mutual support. Such courses, in London and Birmingham for example, have proved effective for access-ing black adults into higher education.

There has been some discussion about whether access courses should be linked to a particular HE programme. Some evidence shows that students from groups suffering high unemployment do value the assurance that successful completion of an access course will guarantee a place on a particular degree course or programme of professional training.

Some single-outlet access courses have developed into multi-exit courses, such that students may progress either into employment or into higher education. The early offerings on social work, education, the social sciences and humanities have been supplemented by vocational and science-based courses. They could be further supplemented by the devel-opment of a framework of national vocational qualifications as proposed by the National Council for Vocational Qualifications (NCVQ) to enable people to acquire credit for structured learning, with clear routes of pro-gression into further and higher education. Severe skills shortages encour-age such developments, which should be monitored for how well they serve black communities. Without this attention to equal opportunities, these initiatives will, like the other vocationally related practices before them (e.g. apprenticeships and youth training schemes), disadvantage black people. For example, will black people be on the less privileged vocational pathways which connect with further rather than higher education and which do not encourage academic study? In 1988, NAB wisely proposed that recruitment on to those courses suffering shortages of students should target underrepresented groups, and that HE institutions should be bound by contractual agreements.

A second thrust of the move to facilitate entry into higher education by non-traditional students focuses on admissions criteria and procedures. The standard admissions procedures are both standardized and competitive; even successful A level entrants may have to be interviewed, for example. In 1980, the CNAA argued that mature students should be judged on individual merit and pointed out that, provided institutions are satisfied that students have the necessary motivation, potential and knowledge to follow a course successfully, then the institutions have the discretion to admit them without formal qualifications.

Ironically, although the setting of hurdles like A levels and the assessment of mature students by academics in interview are meant to ensure equity (in that admission is through merit and achievement and not patronage or connection), complex judgements about competing candidates and discretionary judgements about the merits of individual cases are potentially racist. The gatekeepers are almost all white. They are as open to the PLU (people like us) factor as anyone else; in other words, they favour people like themselves and are likely to make biased judgements about people from different backgrounds to their own. It is possible that discretionary interviews of mature students, a supposedly facilitating device which may work for other groups of mature applicants (say, middle-class white women) could work against black adults. In order for this procedure *not* to be inherently racist, there would need to be more black gatekeepers, effective awareness training for current admissions tutors (which could be organized by departments of adult and continuing education) and targets set and monitored. Or a system of positive discrimination could be devised to ensure that the same proportion of black applicants are successful, relevant to the number of black people who apply, as white applicants. The justification of current practices – both traditional and new – on the basis of equity considerations, is highly problematic.

Finally, the accreditation of prior learning (APL) and of prior experiential learning (APEL) is seen as another route into higher education for mature students. APL involves recognized accreditation of learning which has taken place outside the traditional forums. For example, some HE institutions have begun to extend their accreditation to work-based learning which can be counted towards academic qualifications. APEL involves a move to systematize the recognition of knowledge and skills gained through mature students' reflections on their life experiences.

Currently, Open College Networks (OCN) are being established to assess and credit access, and other second-chance-to-learn courses, across a region. These courses are themselves beginning to systematize advanced standing on the basis of APL and APEL. Clearly, a new expansion of higher education requires a framework of this kind, which allows individual students to acquire and to add to a portfolio of accredited learning so that they can study at their own pace, to suit individual life circumstances, and which allows for more ready transfer from one institution to another. If one were to add to this kind of credit accumulation and transfer (CATS) current moves towards the modularization of courses within higher education, it does begin to seem that a more adult, perhaps one could even say mature, system is evolving. It is not yet the time to be complacent, however. These movements – on the whole, 'grass-roots' initiatives – are in their early stages and are not unproblematic. For example, as Robin Usher (1989) convincingly argues, while the notion of experiential learning is liberating and coherent in its application to mature students, the notion of translating it into behaviouristic competences in order to credit it is more problematic (he locates his unease in epistemological considerations which connect with those discussed in Chapter 8).

In addition, with APL and APEL we again have a movement that will benefit some mature students but which may discriminate against minority ethnic groups in at least two ways. First, as with discretionary interviews, the accreditation will largely be by white (racism-unaware) academics. Second, since experience, and the knowledge gained from reflecting on it, is partly a product of cultural background and tradition, the knowledge and skills of minority ethnic group students may be misassessed against criteria devised solely by a different ethnic group.

# Demolishing the Ivory Tower

Turning from 'big A' to 'little a' access, Woodrow *et al.* (1987) have identified three stages in making institutions more accessible: the decision by an HE institution to become involved with an access initiative, which requires some recognition that non-traditional students would be acceptable; the negotiation of an appropriate curriculum with the external provider, which involves a learning process; and the direct experience of teaching access students. Thus the institution will have more black students *and* a less racist curriculum and ethos.

There is still a boundary, however, around this changed provision. A more radical version of 'little a' access is not that of crossing an alternative boundary to a more accessible provision within, but that of removing the boundary altogether. The boundary which guards the Ivory Tower is not just to be scaled or breached, but destroyed, thereby moving from an elite and competitive model to a mass model of higher education (Tight 1989).

Advocates of changing the nature of higher education in organizational or curriculum terms are also likely to favour a less competitive system. But this need not be so. Given mistaken assumptions about 'maintaining academic standards' (see Chapter 8), an educator might favour institutional change – such as the substantial growth in part-time degrees that we have seen in the last twenty years – within competitive boundaries. Some advocates of opening doors in the walls may wish to keep the current curriculum (as with the Open University). In other words, one may favour keeping, scaling or demolishing some form of entry requirements and one may favour keeping or changing current provision within the institution.

However, it could be argued that open access, and changes of curriculum, ethos and organization, are inextricably connected – each supports and influences the other. Changes of curriculum and ethos are inextricably connected with the radical structural change that boundary demolition would entail. It is neither a case of scaling the walls (as with access courses) to a changed provision, nor demolishing the walls around an unchanged curriculum (as with the Open University[1]), but of demolishing the tower – walls and all.

Griffin (1983) has argued that barriers to access are not resolvable in technical and institutional terms, that access to education is a 'collective and political issue of knowledge and power in society'. As I shall similarly argue in Chapter 9, beyond the meritocratic ideology, of equalizing opportunity in competition for higher education, lies a democratic ideology. The latter suggests that by providing higher education to a much larger and more diverse clientele, we would enrich higher education through the transformation of knowledge itself.

# 8 | Access and Maintaining Academic Standards

## The quality debate

These kinds of proposals about access and accessibility and mainstreaming antiracist continuing education, tend to raise concerns about maintaining academic standards. Quality issues have also been sharpened by the more direct competition between the older and post-1989 universities and by the Jarratt Report (1985), which sought to improve university management. Managers have a keener eye on staff appraisal and 'cost-effectiveness'. Small wonder that 'quality is the flavour of the year in the early nineties' (Duke 1992), as shown by the succession of relevant conferences and projects and by considerable preparations and discussions about visits by the AAU (the academic audit-unit of the CVCP) and about what might follow the old Council for National Academic Awards (CNAA). Add to this that the flavour of the 1980s was the issue of widening access to higher education, and that momentum for action has at last been achieved, then one can appreciate why quality issues are particularly prominent at this time.

There has long been a widely shared assumption that moving towards a mass system of higher education entails a dilution of quality. Peter Scott (1990) has pointed out that the image of an exhaustible 'pool of talent' is deep inside the collective consciousness:

> The resilience of this image in the face of apparent refutation can be explained by the fact that this impression of scarce or, at any rate, limited talent arises not from pragmatic investigation of increasing staying-on rates in school, the rising tide of A levels or the academic success of non-traditional students. The image is not about academic quality at all in a specific sense, although it is fed by grumbles about less literate students. Rather the 'pool of talent' is a cultural construction that reflects a still narrow view of the possibilities of higher

education, perhaps also a fear about the consequences for the present arrangement of society if the opposite were proved to be true. And it is this cultural construction that must be dismantled if the underdevelopment of British higher education is to be successfully overcome.

(Scott 1990: 27–8)

In my own experience, as a member of a department of continuing education, I have found, as no doubt have others similarly placed, that this concern about academic standards arises when the university's adult educators are: (1) seeking to increase access to higher education for educationally 'disadvantaged' groups such as mature students, women, ethnic minorities and students with special needs; (2) seeking to recognize nonformal qualifications for the purpose of entry to, or advanced standing on, graduate and postgraduate courses; (3) seeking to extend the kind of courses available to students in the institution or available to the general public through extramural provision; (4) seeking to extend the forms of teaching available to the students.

But what do people mean by 'academic standards' and how are they best maintained? I will show that 'academic standards' has a number of aspects and examine how these interrelate. I will explore the implications of this analysis for concerns about maintaining standards and argue that the changes I advocate, including those required to widen access to higher education, do *not* threaten academic standards. On the contrary, such changes have considerable potential to raise them and to improve, not dilute, the quality of higher education.

In the kind of discussion to which I have referred, academic standards are taken to be something that academics understand and must protect. Because the meaning of 'academic standards' is taken as self-evident, it is rarely analysed or even defined. Yet it is a complex term which is used to refer to at least *four* distinct, if interrelated, ideas.

1. *Academic standards as academic skills.* Usually (good) 'academic standards' implicitly refers to a high level of second-order analytical skills. University students are not expected to produce purely descriptive work but to look at such descriptive data at one remove – to criticize, analyse and organize it. (Criticism involves detecting the flaws and strengths of one's own and others' arguments and theories. Analysis often involves conceptual clarification. Organization involves finding a fruitful categorization of the first-order data to produce explanatory power and insight.)

   Such analytical skills involve understanding (and at a more advanced level, developing) theoretical frameworks. Analytical frameworks provide concepts and principles by which to interpret and explain first-order data and often draw, but are not founded, on the established academic disciplines. Their 'second-order' nature is characterized by generality of applicability and comprehensiveness of explanation. First-order data are provided by our shared commonsense world which we learn about at school (I do not deny that children can and do also begin to acquire more advanced, second-order skills at school).

2. *Academic standards as academic disciplines.* Good 'academic standards' also implicitly refers to mastery of an established academic discipline or disciplines. The university student is expected to acquire not just any knowledge but to develop an understanding of a particular form of knowledge. These academic disciplines – developed, disciplined, systematic forms of enquiry – involve propositional (knowing that) and skill-based (knowing how) content. Postgraduate students and university staff are perhaps expected to contribute to the further development of their discipline.

3. *Academic standards as good pedagogy.* Here good 'academic standards' implicitly refers to the quality of the teaching and learning interaction. University students should not only achieve particular kinds and levels of learning, but make significant progress. Good teaching can make a crucial contribution to the kind and degree of progress. High academic standards in this context demand that the teaching is appropriate both to the learner and to what is being learned, so that satisfactory learning can take place. 'Teaching' must be understood within a post-modern epistemological framework and incorporate a student-centred approach. This implies that the learning will be satisfying to the student, and be integrated into his or her cognitive repertoire. An interest in the adult learning process is a professional interest for the staff of CE departments *qua* researchers and should be a professional concern for all staff of every department *qua* teachers.

4. *Academic standards as academic virtues.* Frequently, good 'academic standards' implicitly refers to exemplary adherence to the academic virtues. Or, to put this another way, it refers to a commitment to values inherent in the academic disciplines and skills. The university student is expected to come to understand these values; students and staff to practise these virtues. I refer to such things as:

(a) Valuing (and practising) the pursuit of 'worthwhile' knowledge (Peters 1966). Much has been written on what knowledge is worthwhile. It is generally taken to be connected with the development of mind and thus to have intrinsic value and to widen the learner's cognitive perspective. Justification for its pursuit is given in terms of this intrinsic value and interest and not in terms of extrinsic usefulness or what is in one's interest.

(b) Valuing (and submitting to) the pursuit of understanding through systematic disciplined enquiry. This overlaps with, but is perhaps not identical to (a). The emphasis in (a) is on the virtue of contributing to knowledge as a common possession and objective construct (Popper 1979). The emphasis here is on the virtue of taking responsibility for one's own continuing academic development.

(c) Valuing (and manifesting) integrity. Academic integrity takes many forms, e.g. honesty in research findings, participation as a citizen of a community of scholars, acknowledgement of others' contributions, fair assessment of students' work.

(d) Valuing (and practising) academic freedom, as in recognizing the unacceptability of authority as a source of knowledge, or of censorship through fear; guarding the academic's right to research and publish without adverse consequences; maintaining the university's and the individual academic's autonomy, etc.

# A complex notion

Thus, these are four interrelated but distinct aspects of the complex notion of academic standards. What are the concerns about maintaining standards if examined in relation to each? Are these aspects maintained separately or simultaneously? In other words, do they stand or fall together?

In relation to academic skills, the concern about maintaining academic standards is presumably a concern that students develop a high level of analytical ability. In the context of academic skills, 'level of learning' combines a reference to the kind of skills required (second-order) and to the degree of competence in those skills. To maintain academic standards is to demand a high level of competence in these particular second-order abilities. It might be that this sense of academic standards as academic skills is the most useful in terms of distinguishing between schooling and higher education. Further questions that arise in connection with maintaining standards in this sense are: what level of academic skill should degree and post-degree work demand, and how do we measure such skills?

In relation to the academic disciplines, the concern about maintaining academic standards is presumably a concern that students attain sufficient mastery of the discipline they elect to study – sufficient, that is, to contribute to its development. One could ask how far mastery of the academic discipline is the same as, or distinct from, developing a high level of competence in analytical skills. I return to this later, but note here that, in so far as they are not identical, maintaining academic standards will involve both developing academic skills and the competences required by one or more of the academic disciplines. Perhaps this sense of academic standards as academic disciplines is the most useful in terms of distinguishing between further or technical education and higher education. Again we must ask what counts as mastery of a discipline and how we judge its attainment.

In relation to academic standards as good pedagogy, the concern is presumably for a high level of teaching to enable students to achieve the required knowledge, understanding and skills. It could be argued that this is the aspect of maintaining academic standards to which many academics pay least attention, partly because of the common view of HE teaching as equivalent to lecturing (our job title is usually 'lecturer'). Even lecturing is not always very well done – a state of affairs encouraged by the relative status, in universities, of teaching and of research. The status of research is being further encouraged by research selectivity exercises which give the assessment of departmental research output and quality a degree of attention that the assessment of teaching quality rarely receives. In connection with good academic standards as good pedagogy, we might ask how we can measure the connection between teaching strategy and learning outcome to develop more effective pedagogy.

Finally, maintaining academic standards in terms of the academic virtues means that both staff and students should practise these virtues. Although it is presumably in the interests of the general well-being, or the good society, that some capable individuals engage in the pursuit of knowledge and understanding, the undertaking of professional responsibility for this activity is not morally incumbent on any particular individual. Nevertheless, once one accepts *that* professional responsibility, practising the academic virtues becomes a moral responsibility.

How do these four aspects of academic standards, and the task of maintaining them, relate to each other? Academic values, given the nature of values, are likely to permeate each of the other aspects of academic standards. Certainly, there are values built into good pedagogy and there is a values dimension to the pursuit of particular kinds and levels of academic and disciplinary skills. What we should notice, too, is that there are different levels within our four-fold list of academic virtues. There are deeper values underpinning academic integrity and freedom in terms of valuing the pursuit of collective knowledge and individual understanding. That is to say, the valuing of academic integrity and freedom (c and d) partly rests on the valuing of the pursuit of knowledge and understanding (a and b). In this sense, commitment to the pursuit of knowledge and understanding is the fundamental academic value.

It would seem that practising the academic virtues can only be done as an integral part of maintaining academic standards in each of the other three senses. Given that one cannot maintain academic values except as an integral part of maintaining academic standards in the other senses, one might then ask, conversely, could one maintain academic standards in those other senses without practising the academic virtues? Could one pursue knowledge, understanding and pedagogical skills without manifesting the academic virtues?

For me, the mundane answer is 'yes', in that, like any human being, an academic may sometimes behave less well than he or she should. In a more Socratic sense, perhaps it is not possible to maintain academic standards in the first three senses without regard to the values intrinsic to them. Certainly, it is not possible for all academics to be unscrupulous all of the time in relation to the academic virtues and yet to maintain the pursuit of knowledge and understanding.

As with practising the academic virtues, given the nature of teaching, maintaining good standards of pedagogy cannot be done in isolation. Teaching implies that there is something to be learned. Good teaching, in the sense of maintaining academic standards, will entail not only use of effective teaching methods, but also that something appropriate is being taught. Here we see that academic standards as good pedagogy is distinct from academic standards in the other senses, but not separable from them in practice. So, one might teach academic skills and disciplines badly, but one cannot teach well at university level without reference to academic skills and worthwhile knowledge. Moreover, good teaching of the academic disciplines and skills is unlikely to be achieved through lectures alone. Skills acquisition is facilitated by practice. The philosophy student, for example, must engage directly in philosophical dialogue and analysis. (The academic virtues are also more likely to be caught by emulating those tutors that practise rather than teach through talk and chalk.)

We have now seen that academic standards as academic virtues and academic standards as good pedagogy involve distinct senses of 'maintaining academic standards', but that as activities they each interrelate with the other, more fundamental, senses of maintaining academic standards in terms of skills and knowledge. It appears, then, that a key question will be about the relation between academic skills and academic disciplines, a question with considerable epistemological implications.

Are academic skills peculiar to particular disciplines or cross-disciplinary? If the latter, what is the relationship between these cross-disciplinary analytical skills and those inherent in particular disciplines? I suggest that some second-order analytical skills are peculiar to particular disciplines and that some are cross-disciplinary. The cross-disciplinary skills are needed by all students whatever their area of study. There are also analytical skills that are required for interdisciplinary fields of study, such as continuing education itself, which require the ability to draw upon the relevant academic disciplines.

In relation to the traditional academic disciplines, one may envisage the map of knowledge as static and given in nature and finite in its form, or as dynamic and constructed. The former would provide less support for the notion of cross-curricular or interdisciplinary analytical skills and would encourage a positivistic research paradigm. The latter would see some analytical skills as additional to those embodied in the traditional disciplines because it would tend to support ideas of gender- and culture-based cognitive styles and skills and the possibility of developing new forms of knowledge and expertise (see Chapter 6).

## Educational change and maintaining standards

I began by pointing out that concern over maintaining academic standards mostly arises in relation to educational change. In particular, I outlined significant examples of proposed and current changes which engender this kind of concern. But how warranted are the fears about maintaining academic standards in the face of such changes in higher education? In order to answer this question, I want to look at the proposed changes in the light of these discussions about all four aspects of 'academic standards'.

The first proposed change was that of widening access to higher education. Why should this engender fear over academic standards and is this fear justified? The fear seems to be based on the belief that widening access to educationally 'disadvantaged' groups such as women, black people and students with special needs, will entail a lowering of entry requirements and a subsequent drop in academic performance.

Let us first consider the widening of access to higher education in a narrow but important respect – the provision of access courses which enable students to obtain places in HE institutions. Such access courses attract mature students, of whom a high proportion are usually women. They aim to develop the skills required by higher education and to bring students to the requisite entry standard, equivalent to A level GCE. Often, entry to the access course is open, but entry to higher education will require the attainment of high grades and will frequently involve interview at the university too. Thus access students are expected to reach the required standard in relevant skills at the point of HE entry. Their courses are often of an interdisciplinary nature and so are more broadly based across academic disciplines than are A level studies. Certainly at Warwick University, where the progress of mature students has been monitored, they are doing very well.

Mature students in a university tend to have a beneficial effect on curriculum and on pedagogy. Their experience of life and the learning gained from work, travel, marriage, parenthood and so on, enriches their thinking and encourages and improves group discussion and other student-centred teaching approaches. Their commitment to the pursuit of knowledge and understanding has been tested by their having to overcome considerable obstacles in order to be at the university at all.

The second proposed change was that of seeking to recognize non-formal qualifications for entry to, or advanced standing on, graduate or postgraduate courses. This, too, is a way of increasing access, but it recognizes that people who may be 'educationally disadvantaged' in traditional terms may not be educationally disadvantaged in terms of relevant learning. The fear, as with access courses, is that *changes* at the point of HE entry may represent a *lowering* of academic skills at the same time and so potentially of subsequent performance. The essential feature of non-formal qualifications is that they should represent *genuine* and relevant skills. Experience in community work, say, could have provided the opportunity to develop and demonstrate a range of analytical skills (e.g. report writing, analysis of client problems, research and critical evaluation of current provision). The much wider range of students, in terms of socio-economic background, ethnicity and experience, drawn in through such recognition, has a beneficial impact on HE pedagogy and encourages the development of non-formal teaching modes.

Perhaps even more significant is the potential for the central academic task – the pursuit of collective and objective knowledge. If we recognize that knowledge is socially constructed and objectivity is to be understood in terms of inter-subjective agreement, then diversity of the potential constructors is a substantial gain for promoting academic standards. A greater range of academic skills and new modes of disciplined enquiry could be collectively developed. An academic body which represents a greater range of perspectives makes this creative epistemological expansion more likely.

Since diversity of perspective enhances the construction of knowledge, could higher education incorporate the perspectives (and thus the interests) of all oppressed groups? Could those with learning disabilities benefit from, and contribute to, higher education? (Similarly, the notion of mass higher education raises the question of whether these are limits to those who could benefit. Is higher education for all?) There are a number of important points here. First, it is my view that we grossly miscalculate the proportion of people who could benefit from 'second-order' or 'higher' learning, partly because we restrict our teaching methods to those which best suit certain sorts of learners. Second, learning disability should not be reified. It is not a blanket condition but a label applied to vulnerable individuals who lack certain abilities relative to the norm but who nevertheless possess a wide range of abilities and disabilities. Some of these individuals would be able to benefit from higher education. Third, those who cannot benefit have their own shared experience of oppression and a distinctive perspective which should be given a 'voice' in HE knowledge constructing research.

Let me illustrate this by reference to Gilligan's discovery of a distinct voice coming out of women's experience (see Chapter 9). On a much more personal level, I have recognized a distinctive voice in those labelled mentally deficient. My 'mentally handicapped' daughter Jane often teaches me new ways of comprehending the world. For example, when she was quite young, my brother Eddie lived in a flat at the top of our house and her cat once shat in his bath. We thought Jane ought to clean up the mess because it had been made by her cat; Jane thought Eddie should clean it up because it was his bath. At first, I thought she was 'missing the point', but as we discussed the situation I became aware of a distinct and alternative moral perspective – the view of one who *controlled* events less than I did but was subject to them more than I was. From this position, one develops a coping strategy whereby one deals with phenomena as best one can, as they arise. From a moral point of view, one does not shirk from chores that arise in the flux of events and need to be done, as Eddie appeared to be doing.

From this (and similar) incidents, I was able to glimpse how forms of rational argument are partly based on one's interests as reflected in one's *competences*. Institutional practices are largely constructed (in addition to the interests and competences of those who control them) on the average competences of most people, and consequently disempowering of those deficient in certain abilities. What I want to say here is that those people – much *fewer* than we suppose – whose abilities are such that they cannot benefit from higher education as *students*, should have a *voice* in the processes by which knowledge is constructed. It is the responsibility of those in higher education, who have accepted the role of knowledge seekers, to devise ways of incorporating disempowered voices in their research and debates.

This view rests on an epistemological thesis, outlined in Chapter 9, which recognizes that knowledge is a human practice and that the non-empirical determinants have implications for the research agenda. This can be contrasted with a view of knowledge as *based* on empirical, simply given in experience, foundations.

As previously mentioned, another proposed change which raises fears about academic standards is the provision of new kinds of courses. It gives rise to the fear that such courses will fail to meet academic criteria. Apart from the fact that, as indicated in the previous paragraph, the notion of academic criteria is less fixed and unproblematic than is perhaps being assumed here, the construction of new academic skills and of new forms of knowledge will positively require new kinds of courses.

Within university extramural programmes, I would also argue that even where a course has little or no academic content, it may yet be justifiable. An enjoyable and effective experience of learning on a craft course, for instance, may build the confidence of students and thus act as a stepping stone to the 'academic' core of the extramural and other university provisions.

The fourth proposed change was the development of new forms of teaching. These tend to meet with initial suspicion, sometimes expressed as a concern about academic standards. Yet the greater the repertoire of teaching approaches, the more successful the learning is likely to be. The most appropriate teaching approach for a particular subject and students can be selected, and interest maintained, because of the wider variety of learning activity. Flexibility of provision also encourages wider participation in higher education. At the present time, there is much interest in distance education. There seems to me no reason to suppose that this approach to teaching and learning (if supplemented by opportunities for discussion and dialogue) cannot produce the required skills, discipline, mastery, progress and virtues.

In short, what I am suggesting is that it is *not* the case that the kinds of changes in higher education that increase participation in it entail, as is often suggested, that academic standards must suffer. Nor are they likely to do so. There is no good reason to fear that they will fail to be maintained, whether we consider academic standards in the sense of analytical skills, or mastery of the existing disciplines, or effective pedagogy, or the academic virtues. Indeed, given the nature of knowledge as a human practice and an interpersonally agreed construct, a wider and more diverse participation in the pursuit of knowledge is likely to produce a more exciting and rapid epistemological advance. Of course, that epistemological advance will involve supplementing and transforming the existing disciplines. It is this consequence of a wider and more diverse clientele that the traditionalists fear. Those who recognize (at whatever level of consciousness) that their own interests are tied to preserving and reproducing existing knowledge are those who wish to maintain the existing elitist *status quo*. By excluding people whose interests are not served by an elitist system, we simultaneously lose the opportunity for a more just (antiracist) mass higher education and for greater epistemological achievements. One of the main claims of this book is that a greater ethnic diversity of students and teachers in any HE system, engaged with a multicultural curriculum and action-oriented research, would more fully realize this epistemological potential. Such changes, therefore, have the potential to *raise* academic standards in terms of skills, of transforming the disciplines and of pedagogy.

Finally, in relation to the academic virtues, wider participation in higher education will bring the familiar mix of exceptionally scrupulous and sometimes less conscientious students and colleagues. The advance here is in terms of the values and virtues of the system as a whole. There is a sense in which the integrity of higher education, and genuine academic freedom, demand a less elitist provision. In this sense, valuing academic standards entails creating a system of higher education that gives learning opportunities to many more people and that provides a voice for all.

# 9 | Inreach: Accessibility and the Antiracist University

The defining tasks of higher education – research and teaching – take place within a particular institutional setting. What, then, will be the nature of research, pedagogy, curriculum and university organization within the mature and antiracist institution? Or, to ask the same question in a less abstract form, if the university is indeed to be accessible to a diverse academic community, comprising adults of all ages drawn from all social and ethnic groups, what implications does this have for what it should be like?

## Higher education and antiracist research

### Revolutionary and normal research

Unlike a market survey, in the context of higher education, research is not just a matter of collecting information but of developing our shared understanding through contributing to, or transforming, our second-order disciplined forms of knowledge.

For any form of knowledge we can distinguish between the content and the form of enquiry. The form of enquiry produces the (provisional) content. An academic who has mastered a discipline makes use of its forms of enquiry and, through insightful analysis of the data produced, adds both to our collective understanding and to the content of the discipline. To modify the form of enquiry is to transform knowledge. An academic who changes a discipline in this way makes a fundamental contribution. In Kuhnian terms, this is 'revolutionary' as distinct from 'normal' research and changes the 'paradigms' which determine what is to count as fact.

Both kinds of research can make an antiracist contribution to a discipline. For example, British history may omit or distort the social contributions of black individuals, and research about such persons adds to the content of history. However, it is when historians grasp (and change) the ways in which their subject may preclude a full understanding of the historical roots of racism through its very forms of enquiry (say, in adopting a 'great man' approach) that history as a discipline is transformed.

## A post-modernist research model

Traditional (positivist) models of research do conceptualize it in terms of accumulating ready-made objective facts. This rests on a realist (foundationalist) epistemology incompatible with the ideas and arguments of this book, which would rather presuppose a constructivist (post-modernist) account of the nature of knowledge.

We construct our knowledge. This knowledge is of a reality structured by categories which are determined by human interests. These interests determine our key concepts, the truth criteria for what will count as a fact, the values that will be fundamental and thus justificatory, the principles that will determine 'rational' argument, and the way in which these elements are structured into methods of enquiry that will be validated as objective forms of knowledge. Such human interests may be universal interests relating to the human condition. Sometimes, however, the development of knowledge may reflect partisan interests, deriving from the power of the dominant group. The former give rise to aspects of knowledge that relate to what is of benefit to everyone and the latter to what is in the interest of those with power.

The relation between knowledge and power has been explored by sociologists and educational theorists such as M.F.D. Young (1971) and M.W. Apple (1982). What counts as knowledge is determined by those who have control – in a capitalist society, those who control the means of production. (Our racist society produces knowledge that is in the interest of the white indigenous majority and, being sexist, male-dominated knowledge too.) To democratize knowledge will require that a greater diversity of knowledge-makers represent the full range of interest groups. Because knowledge is not produced through the apprehension of an a-historic and neutral reality, and is not based on given foundations, but is a human construct influenced by power relations and ideology, democratic construction requires more inclusive participation in the collective task.[1]

Usher and Bryant (1989), in their examination of the interrelationship between theory, practice and research in adult education, give an account of action research which exemplifies this constructivist epistemology. Traditional models of research are said to rest on realist core assumptions: that there is an 'objective' and well-founded real world external to and independent of individuals and that knowledge of this world can be discovered empirically using proper methods and procedures. This common-sense view of knowledge is based on a correspondence theory of truth, a cumulative account of science and a foundationalist conception of theory, and is rightly problematized. As they point out, even natural science is no longer based on naive realism. The post-empiricist work of Kuhn and others provides an account of scientific knowledge as socially constructed. And if knowledge is not simply achieved by discovering 'out there' facts, then this has implications for research – for how knowledge is individually and collectively achieved.

It is individually achieved as we form and transform our individual meaning perspectives. Because these are *meaning* perspectives, they are achieved through a social process, although they represent the manifestation of an individual mind. The individual acquires *interpersonally* agreed concepts and forms of thought. When we transform our meaning perspective in a unique way, to be valid (i.e. meaningful) the transformation must be capable of eliciting interpersonal agreement. If the transformation is sufficiently powerful, it may influence collective meaning and thus become part of our objective forms of knowledge.

## Forms of knowledge

Given constructivism, the traditional developed academic disciplines are not *the* only possible forms of knowledge. For example, over time, a form of knowledge could be differentially transformed to give us alternative forms of enquiry. Interdisciplinary studies also produce new knowledge and skills that are not always locatable in one of the academic disciplines. Practical fields of study like continuing education also produce their own form of knowledge. Just as the disciplines are not founded on an a-historical reality, they are not themselves fixed foundations upon which practical interdisciplinary fields of study are based. Here learning comes through practice and the purpose of theorizing is to improve practice. [The collection of papers edited by Barry Bright (1989) on *Theory and Practice in the Study of Adult Education* focus on the relationship between adult education and the disciplines. Interestingly, this raised 'deep epistemological issues not anticipated' about the epistemological status of the disciplines themselves.] I earlier gave an account of continuing education in terms of transforming individual meaning perspectives through engaging in social action against oppression, and thus reconciling liberal and radical traditions. Higher education research into continuing education would study this process to yield new knowledge about it. Again the knowledge is validated in terms of contributing to the improvement of practice.

Given this account of the nature of knowledge, it is the case that it will have been differently constructed in some ways over time within the various cultural traditions. Human interests have varied (within limits) in different societies and thus differently influenced the shared meaning perspectives of the ethnic groups within them. Transformation of human knowledge will be facilitated if this diversity of perspectives enriches the collective task. Diversity of voice and interests will stimulate existing forms of knowledge and will also extend what counts as worthwhile and objective.[2] Through the synthesis of elements from different cultural traditions, new forms of knowledge will emerge over time. The possibility of cultural synthesis multiplies the developmental and transformational epistemological possibilities.

## A feminist perspective

Within most cultural traditions, the powerless position of women relative to men has impoverished the construction of knowledge. Feminist scholarship has sought to incorporate and develop knowledge for and about women. Women's studies developed in the 1970s as an independent specialization. Women also sought to have the knowledge so generated incorporated into the mainstream of disciplinary teaching and research. Many disciplines had 'pathologized' women, who were portrayed in a stereotyped manner. Feminist research revealed male bias, a bias which influenced what subjects were studied, how data were collected and how research was conceptualized. Gail Kelly and Carolyn Korsmeyer (1991) have examined the relationship between feminist scholarship and the academic disciplines and shown how disciplinary assumptions were challenged in history, anthropology and education. Feminist scholarship went beyond critiques to forge new forms of enquiry, albeit shaped by the academic disciplines that had been criticized. It was influenced by a variety of theoretical movements and is thus not monolithic but full of tensions and debates. It has challenged HE pretences to neutrality and has conceptualized research as action-oriented and tied to liberating women.

Ethnicity considerations are relevant here in two distinct ways. First, Western feminist scholarship has recognized its own racism in tending to exclude the voices of black women – voices bringing perspectives developed through the experience of racism and which draw on 'other' cultural traditions. Second, with the possibility of cultural synthesis, we can see how the generation of knowledge could escape the confines of the traditional disciplines. When we criticize the disciplines as feminist, we both transform and remain tied to them. Cultural synthesis which reconciles culturally distinct forms of knowledge could not only transform these, but produce new ones.

## Enriching academic research

It might be useful at this point to consider some concrete examples of how our collective understanding can be enriched by a diversity of perspectives and by cultural synthesis. For the former, I use an important feminist example, and I set the latter in the practical field of education.

Kohlberg's influential account of moral development, which has been widely accepted as an important contribution to developmental psychology, has been much enriched by the work of Carol Gilligan. Gilligan recognized that developmental theories have been built on observations of men's lives and so had failed to understand women's psychology and women's interests. Her work as a developmental psychologist therefore focused on women's moral judgements, and she discovered a new way of speaking about moral problems:

> It was then that I began to notice the recurrent problems in interpreting women's development and to connect these problems to the repeated exclusion of women from the critical theory-building studies of psychological research.
>
> (Gilligan 1982: 1)

Put briefly, Gilligan discovered the importance of an ethic of care taking more account of context, in women's developing moral judgements, as distinct from Kohlberg's focus on justice and rules. The difference in theme was based on empirical observation through her work with women, but she had discovered a distinction between two modes of thought rather than an absolute difference in the moral judgements of women and men. Women as well as men make use of both modes of thought, but tend to do so in different degrees. Thus data and reflection on women's experiences generated a new theory which potentially yields a more encompassing view of the lives of both sexes.

We see in Gilligan's work how her feminist perspective has enriched our collective knowledge and understanding. It is no accident that this powerful new perspective on moral development came from the research of a female academic. Carol Gilligan sees what she did as supportive of a constructivist epistemology:

> This discovery occurs when theories formerly considered to be sexually neutral in their scientific objectivity are found instead to reflect a consistent observational and evaluative bias. Then the presumed

neutrality of science, like that of language itself, gives way to the recognition that the categories of knowledge are human constructions. The fascination with point of view that has informed fiction in the twentieth century and the corresponding recognition of the relativity of judgement infuse our scientific understanding as well when we begin to notice how accustomed we have become to seeing life through men's eyes.

(Gilligan 1982: 6)

Gilligan also claims, like William Perry, that the abandonment of absolutes which can occur in the course of intellectual and ethical development during the early adult years is accompanied by a move towards tolerance. (The encouragement of this abandonment by young adults at university could thus be seen as a contribution to antiracist and anti-sexist education through the development of a tolerant disposition.)

To apprehend that there are two contexts for moral development encourages both sexes to understand that moral judgement is contextually relative, and leads to a greater appreciation of both points of view and to less misunderstanding. More specifically, women and men will recognize the need to mitigate justice with mercy (care) and the importance of caring not only for the other, but also (in justice, and as women tend to neglect) for the self.

Gilligan's important research not only added to the content of developmental psychology, but highlighted a new mode of thinking about moral issues. It was more contextualized and less hierarchical thinking than Kohlberg's theory had recognized. Given a moral problem, it encouraged not an either/or choice of solutions but the finding of an inclusive (synthesizing) answer to moral dilemmas. (Perhaps 'feminist' forms of thought may *tend* to be associative, rather than hierarchical as in stage theories; particularized rather than abstract, as with the development of learning through stories and biography; and synthesizing rather than dialectical.)

An example of cultural synthesis in education could be provided by the current controversy about separate schools, which partly arises from competing perspectives on pluralism itself. Should there be separate state-funded Christian, Jewish and Muslim schools or should all children be educated together? The Swann Report (1985, on the education of minority ethnic children) advocated an integrated education for all children based on shared values in common schools. One Muslim response (Cambridge Islamic Academy 1986) advocated separate education based on Islamic culture and values. Each model of education could be seen as fair and appropriate for a multicultural society. The former, which could be called 'integrational pluralism', is appropriate in that all children are educated together and offered a pluralist curriculum, and the latter, which could be called 'dynamic pluralism', is seen as appropriate precisely because it allows for the preservation of all cultural traditions with the different groups sharing in social development from positions of religious identity and strength (Skinner 1990). A compromise, which in practice *synthesizes* these perspectives on pluralism, might be to develop provision such that each child whose parents so wished would receive both integrated (mainstream) and segregated (own community-based) state-funded learning sessions in a new, flexible model of education for a multicultural society.

Young Pai (1990) has given an account of lifelong learning that is based on the idea of synthesis, which he calls syncretism, and which is not dissimilar to what I have said about collective knowledge and individual meaning perspectives. Pai himself makes the Mezirow connection. To live most effectively, to achieve one's objectives, one needs to know about other cultural traditions. 'Syncretism is the reconciliation of two or more cultural systems or elements, with the modification of both.' Our knowledge of other cultures becomes integrated into our private culture.

> Multicultural education should be seen as the process by which each individual can learn to live in a progressively effective and enriching way by acquiring cognitive understanding and significant experiences of a wide range of cultural patterns. Thus, a primary objective of multicultural education should be the increase of the individual's private cultural repertoire in his/her private culture, as well as developing the skill with which one can reconcile divergent patterns so that a new and unique approach to life may emerge. This should indeed be a central goal of lifelong learning.
>
> (Pai 1990: 25)

Thus, through cultural synthesis (or syncretism), a pluralist curriculum can enrich both individual learning and the collective generation of human knowledge.

These brief examples of feminist scholarship and cultural synthesis illustrate how a greater diversity among teachers and learners in higher education will enhance higher education in two ways. It will extend the learning of individuals as they develop their meaning perspectives through dialogue and debate which is enriched by the diversity of the participants. Also, it will augment the research that is done – constructing objective knowledge through extending, transforming and synthesizing the forms of knowledge that have already been achieved. A system of higher education in which minority ethnic groups (and women from all groups) had a more representative and powerful part, and in which a multicultural curriculum was being offered and developed, would be a higher education enriched in its central tasks of teaching and research.

## Race-related research

Higher education research on race, in whatever domain (social welfare, education, law, etc.) raises several ethical issues. These arise partly because the subject being researched involves unequal power relationships; and here too race can act as a barium meal in revealing issues with a more general (equal opportunities) applicability. Because of group inequalities of power, the researcher must act responsibly in relation to the well-being of relatively powerless groups and individuals. I remember, for example, that when I was working in Handsworth, my own and several other voluntary organizations were 'researched'. As a result, an eminent academic published the name of a black activist who had been critical of the police. This was irresponsible. (The demand that we reference or support every claim is sometimes a symptom of a false positivistic notion of objectivity. There are occasions when the reader must simply test out what is claimed by comparing it against his or her own experience of oppression.)

To act responsibly in relation to inequalities of power will entail not pathologizing black communities and not hurting black individuals. Thus Carrington and Short (1992) have criticized much research with young children for both reinforcing stereotypes of black groups and for hurting the feelings of black (and white) children. Similarly, Harbhaja Singh Brar (1992) argues that since value-free research is not possible, research projects should not reproduce racism but oppose it. At the individual level, he maintains that black people are sometimes exploited as researchers being used, when in a junior post, to gain *access* to minority communities while more senior white researchers subsequently appropriate 'credit' for the (sometimes damaging) research that is done. He draws attention to a number of ethical dilemmas that may confront the responsible race researcher: dealing with racist incidents that occur; deciding on confidentiality in connection with information on racist practice; considering whether the antiracist ends justify some dubious means; and whether to be honest about one's antiracist ends and views.

What, then, will a responsible and antiracist research project be like? Clearly, such a project should not pathologize black groups. Much research spotlights minority groups rather than the racism of the wider society. The research assumption should be that racial discrimination is a central factor in race relations: white racism is the problem, not black people. A positivistic research model encourages the reproduction of knowledge through the accumulation of 'facts'. This will reproduce racist myths and assumptions. Antiracist research will be action-oriented in seeking to transform, not reproduce, social reality. Such action research will actively involve oppressed groups (and the ethnicity of the researcher has been known to influence face-to-face interviews, and thus may sometimes be an issue). Academics cannot become the voice of the oppressed. People represent their own interests best. In enlightened research, black and white academics will collaborate with, and be accountable to, those whose oppressed situation the action research is designed to redress.

# Higher education and antiracist teaching

## Teaching as good practice

Teaching that is approved of is sometimes referred to as good practice. What do educators mean by 'good practice', and what would good anti-racist practice be like? We need to distinguish between good practice that refers to the quality of the teaching/learning interaction and process, and good practice that refers more broadly to practices in the education system which are conducive to, or establish the conditions for, good teaching and learning to take place. Thus NIACE (1989) has argued that a system suited to adult learners must make continuing education central to the higher education system and give attention to many elements of institutional policy – recruitment, needs analysis and outreach, publicity, selection procedures, prior qualifications and experiences, curriculum change, access routes, collaborative systems, access to assessment, physical access, student support, financial access, planning and implementation, guidance, course structure, funding, marketing and staff development.

Similarly, we could distinguish between good antiracist practice in terms of the antiracist dimensions of the teaching and learning process and good antiracist practice more broadly, in relation to ensuring that all the policies, structures and practices in the education system are such as to eliminate racial discrimination. It is with the quality of the teaching and learning interaction that I am concerned in this section.

Good teaching will facilitate the achievement of educational aims and good antiracist teaching the achievement of antiracist educational aims. In a sense, good antiracist teaching is an aspect of good teaching *per se*. 'Good racist teaching' is a contradiction in terms. 'Good' carries the double implication that such practice connects with worthwhile outcomes ('good' in its ethical sense) and that such practice is effective in relation to these educational ends ('good' in the more pragmatic, efficiency sense). Thus teaching that represents good practice will effectively facilitate the achievement of educational aims and objectives. It is not good practice if anti-educational (e.g. indoctrinatory), unethical (e.g. intrinsically unfair, as through racial bias) or ineffective (e.g. technically incompetent).

Antiracist teaching, then, refers to teaching that is based on anti-racist educational aims. Thus teaching based on a curriculum that was ethnocentric, or a teaching approach that was racially discriminatory, would not be antiracist teaching. Antiracist teaching could also refer to a particular teaching approach – a radical pedagogy – through which antiracist knowledge and understanding is constructed (Giroux 1992). Good teaching for adults has been characterized as arising from the nature of adult learning, and called 'androgogy' (Knowles 1970). Clearly, good antiracist teaching will be based on the nature of adult learning *and* have antiracist educational aims. What follows explores first the notion of androgogy, and then antiracist teaching in more direct and specific senses.

## Androgogy and good teaching

We have seen that the notion of antiracist good practice in education interrelates the ideas of effective teaching with that of antiracist aims. Good and effective teaching of *adults* has been thought to require in addition that the nature of adult students be taken into account. For example, adult students bring distinctive experiences to their learning, often combined with some lack of confidence in their academic abilities. Adult educators therefore make claims such as:

> Good adult education practice starts from where students are, from the experience and skills they bring to their learning. Since these experiences are diverse and their starting points different learning groups need to have a plurality of learning and teaching strategies, and the negotiation of what is to be learned, and in what way, is critical to making the process shared.
>
> (Tuckett 1990)

These kinds of factors, thought to be relevant to adult learning (previous experience, negotiation, active problem-solving approaches, etc.) are sometimes collectively referred to as 'androgogy' (the teaching/learning of adults) (Knowles 1970) and distinguished from 'pedagogy' (the teaching/learning of children). It is not always clear if androgogy is meant to be a theory about how adults learn best or a value-based exhortation about how they ought to be taught, but in any case this distinction between the learning of adults and children is problematic.

The distinction fails to hold as an account of how things *are* done, since both kinds of teaching occur in both sectors, but it also fails to hold as a theory about the different nature of learning in children and adults. Effective teaching of both (as good primary school teachers know) takes account of the students' previous experiences and current interests and actively engages the learner. Even the non-voluntary nature of schooling is not as clear-cut a difference in relation to effective learning as might be supposed. Some adults do not have much real choice about attendance either. For example, some young people attend youth training schemes in order to remain in receipt of benefit. Some adults are on courses because these are the only means of entry to a particular job or to promotion. Again, the point is that reluctant attenders of any age are more likely to learn if the teaching approach adopted succeeds in engaging their participation in an activity.

Similarly, understood simply as a prescription to teach students with respect and *as if* autonomous and rational, androgogy has force in both sectors. If children are not so treated, how are they to become rational and autonomous? It is small wonder that some adults are put off continuing their education due to negative memories of school. My purpose in touching on the distinction between pedagogy and androgogy is that an exploration of the features commonly ascribed to each is helpful in considering teaching against racism.

Teaching in higher education has traditionally been based on lectures delivered by an authority imparting his (usually) knowledge. For some learners who are abstract thinkers and who readily absorb abstract ideas, this works well for many subjects, although not for the kind of understanding involved in 'conscientization', including conscientization to racism (Freire 1970). For other learners, teaching approaches that present the material to be understood in more concrete and specific forms are more effective for *any* material.

Although good teaching is thus context-dependent, and selects the approach most suited to the material and to the learners in a given situation, over a longer programme some *variety* of technique will usually be more effective. This variety will be more effective for three reasons: first, the class will probably include individuals who between them have a range of learning styles; second, the material to be covered will usually include propositional and skill-based knowledge, with both relatively impersonal and more attitude/emotion-engaging dimensions; and, third, variety is likely to be more stimulating. Sameness of approach may begin to bore. This is fatal to the particular learning in progress and simultaneously provides a negative lesson about learning itself. In higher education, therefore, as in other sectors, lecturing is insufficient as the *sole* teaching method; it is particularly ineffective for some kinds of learning, such as understanding racism.

Teaching against racism aims to facilitate the development of individual meaning perspectives which incorporate positive racial attitudes. Attitudinal changes, as I have argued, are not readily achieved through 'talk and chalk'. Students passively listening to a lecture on racism are not likely to examine or change their own prejudiced assumptions and stereotypes. Learning based on active participation through discussion, which draws on students' shared experiences, which is experiential and reflective (through role play and experiential exercises such as those devised by Katz 1978) and which facilitates direct encounter and dialogue with the views and experiences of black students, is more likely to lead to an internalization of knowledge about racism, and a commitment to oppose it.

In short, for all learners, androgogical approaches to teaching against racism are more effective. At any age, experiential learning and a non-authoritarian approach are more likely to change prejudiced attitudes and to generate a commitment to oppose racism, to encourage the development of further critical awareness and to affect behaviour.

## Antiracist teaching

Mind is not simply a pre-existing vessel for the passive reception of fixed truths, but could be said to come into being through the making of meaning,[3] so the learning involved in acquiring knowledge (i.e. in developing one's personhood through the construction of meaning) is an active process which requires involvement with other persons.

Within shared discussion, the asymmetrical power relation between teacher and taught is redefined to allow students to draw on their own experience as real knowledge. They can explore how power works in the discourse and practices of daily life and the felt oppressions of the discussants (they can similarly explore how texts express different ideological interests, including racist ideology, and deconstruct them). Such a learning process legitimizes the students' experiences and backgrounds. Differences in experiences and backgrounds provide an opportunity to have varied voices in the learning conversation and for students to see that there are different ways of perceiving the world. Without this pluralism of voice, fewer categories of meaning and fewer possibilities of experience are incorporated into the knowledge they collectively create and individually acquire.[4] This could be described as a radical pedagogy through which antiracist knowledge is constructed. It presupposes the constructivist epistemology outlined in the previous discussion about research and the acquisition of knowledge.[5]

To sum up, good teaching, from primary through to higher education, will adopt approaches which embody egalitarian values and respect for the students' prior experience and learning, and potential autonomy ('good' in its ethical sense) and which employs a variety of experiential techniques ('good' in the sense of effective). It is particularly important that these values and techniques inform practice when the 'holy ground' between teacher and taught engages the whole person (as in racism awareness) emotionally as well as cognitively, and seeks to influence behaviour as well as ideas. In learning about oppression, students draw on their own experience in a shared discussion to generate deeper understanding for all the participants.

Young children are in the process of forming attitudes. There is evidence that even *very* young children have already internalized social prejudices about race (Milner 1983). Nevertheless, since in adulthood racial prejudice is often entrenched, in this sense the adult educator might be thought to have the more difficult task.

# Higher education and an antiracist curriculum

Direct teaching about racism, or antiracist pedagogy, is only one specific part of the general need to permeate the curriculum with an antiracist (as well as a lifelong) perspective. For each syllabus, tutors need to dismantle the current ethnocentricity which occurs from the *commission* of use of racist material, and the *omission* of a black perspective. Many courses and learning resources are infected by racist bias, assumptions and use of language. Several are also ethnocentric due to the total omission of 'other' cultural values, race issues, or reference to black achievement and oppression. An antiracist curriculum will be such that the critical skills taught enable students to detect racial bias, the knowledge gained will incorporate a global dimension and the understanding developed will include an educated awareness of oppression in its various historical and contemporary forms.

A survey into antiracist practice in higher education (see Chapter 7) revealed some examples of this kind. One history department, for example, teaches students to examine sources and secondary works critically and to be aware of the assumptions built into them, not least in relation to the difficulties of perception and interpretation in studying the history of European empires; incorporates material to increase awareness of the diversity of cultures and the achievements of non-European societies; and includes reading and study about oppressive systems such as slavery and apartheid.

It is not necessary for each academic to start from scratch in developing an antiracist and pluralist curriculum in her/his subject. There are curricular and resource exemplars and checklists, incorporating principles of good practice and syllabus suggestions for almost all areas of the university curriculum (for information and advice, see the post-school antiracist resource list in Appendix 1). It remains necessary, however, to select what is appropriate in one's own work, and to develop an antiracist and pluralist perspective appropriate to one's own *particular* course: its syllabus, aims, content, learning materials and teaching methodology.

I have made reference to both 'antiracist' and 'pluralist' curriculum development, conjoining these terms, because in my view it is important to ensure that teaching about and against racism includes, and is supported by, a cultural pluralism of content, values and assumptions. However, antiracism and multiculturalism are not always thus taken to be mutually supportive and overlapping, but rather seen as dichotomous and ideologically irreconcilable. Antiracist education, but not multiculturalism, is seen as concerned with countering institutional discrimination arising from inequalities of race and class. Racism perpetuates the unequal power relations between groups in society and must be challenged by overtly political action to produce radical change in the education system itself.

In 1985, Grinter sought to bridge this divide between multicultural and antiracist education. He recognized the need for pluralism in the curriculum *and* the elimination of discriminatory institutional practices. Troyna (1987) and others have claimed that this fails to recognize the 'irreconcilable ideological differences' between the two approaches – the liberal reformist approach of multiculturalism and the radical militant stance of antiracism. The debate continues into the new era with, I think, a regrettable potential for dividing natural allies (liberals and radicals) in joint resistance to a conservative monocultural education, as reflected in the National Curriculum's emphasis on British history and the Christian religion, for example, and in their joint struggle to eliminate racial prejudice and discrimination in and through education.

Following and supporting Grinter, I have argued that the putative dichotomy between multicultural and antiracist education is misconceived. Provided that the pluralism in the curriculum is genuine and thoroughgoing (i.e. not tokenistic), then it makes an antiracist contribution. Thus one form of multicultural education is necessary but not sufficient for antiracist education – necessary because it tackles cultural racism in the curriculum but insufficient because antiracism must address the issue of structural discrimination too. This antiracist form of multicultural education (or new multiculturalism) recognizes an overlap rather than a dichotomy between multicultural and antiracist education.

Table 2 provides a brief comparative description of the characteristics that tend to be associated with multicultural and antiracist education, particularly in the debate about the 'two currents' (Hatcher 1987).[6] Initially, multicultural education focused on the content of the curriculum, but 'new multiculturalism' has recognized the importance of institutional racism too. Similarly, in recent years, 'antiracist' education has been developed to take account of criticisms about the lack of curriculum substance and of explicit strategy suggestions in relation to its political goals (ibid.).

Surely now, in the 1990s, we have reached a point such that further polarization between multiculturalists and antiracists will be damaging to the progress of antiracist change. There is considerable overlap in the perspectives. Any particular educator may value both individual autonomy and justice for oppressed groups; pluralism in the curriculum and anti-racist teaching, and so on. If egalitarian changes are to be achieved in the era of the Education Reform Act, then we need as large a group of educators as possible, to unite against conservative and reactionary forces intent on preventing genuinely pluralist and antiracist developments. The real enemies of 'new multiculturalists' and 'antiracists' are those who are intent on preserving the racist *status quo*. Moreover, all those who want educational change need to work for it at both the curriculum and institutional levels, and with a variety of strategies and projects, including the development of a curriculum that is culturally plural, as an aspect of anti-racist education.

# Higher education and antiracist university organization

In *Process and Structure in Higher Education*, Becher and Kogan (1992) outline a model of higher education comprising the four main levels of the system – central authority, institution, basic unit and individual – and explore their interconnections. They also describe four ideologies, 'quadrilateral of interests, and each emphasizing their own value positions', which influence the values and practices at all main levels: professional values, management values, market values and social utility.

The ideology of *professional values* they associate with a small and elite system. This university ideal is that of an institution independent of resource constraints and thus able to set its own objectives and research agenda. Such an institution would not be organized in a management hierarchy but as a collegium whose autonomy is justified in terms of higher education's task – the generation of knowledge.

Becher and Kogan contrast this traditional ideology of autonomy with that of accountable management. They suggest that *management values* can contribute to the good running of HE systems and institutions (and are presumably justified in these terms), but can also become a 'pathological obstruction' in conflict with academic norms.

Forcefully promoted by a right-wing government, *market values* have strongly emerged. For the university in this scenario, funding will be bid for competitively and also secured by the selling of their services on the open market. Justification is in terms of the need for a highly educated workforce. Expansion would be funded through this kind of competitive privatization as academics become entrepreneurs. As with management values, these market values could damage good research and teaching, particularly in the humanities, the critical social sciences and the theoretical basis of science and technology.

**Table 2** Multicultural and 'antiracist' education: Distinguishing characteristics

| Aspects | Multicultural education | Antiracist education |
|---|---|---|
| Ideology | *Liberal* (individual autonomy and rights) <br> – wider spectrum of views <br> – reformist, incremental change | *Radical* (class analysis of racism) <br> – more homogeneous (Marxist) <br> – require revolution to overthrow capitalism |
| Values | *Freedom* – of individual thought and action | *Liberation* – justice for oppressed groups |
| Goals | *Intercultural understanding* <br> – reduction of prejudice among individuals <br> *Limited social reform* <br> – that which is possible through education | *Unequal group power redress* <br> – removing institutional discrimination <br> *Radical social change* <br> – a realistic educational goal |
| Curriculum | *Liberal education* <br> – emphasis on individual educational development <br> – PSMEd (personal, social and moral education) <br> *Pluralism* <br> – focus on 'other cultures' <br> – implicit antiracism/anti-ethnocentricity <br> – social and cultural aspects | *Education as social action* <br> – emphasis on institutional change <br> – political education through social action <br> *Antiracism* <br> – focus on racism of dominant culture <br> – explicit antiracist teaching <br> – economical and political aspects |
| Pedagogy | *To promote individual development* <br> – psychology of the learning process | *To promote political action* <br> – sociology: the influence of school/social structures on the learning process |

| | | |
|---|---|---|
| **Change strategy** | *Change locus*: school<br>1. Rational persuasion and debate<br>2. Reformist<br>3. Means *and* ends morally important<br>4. Removing barriers to facilitate equal opportunities for individuals regardless of race or gender | *Change locus*: wider political structures and alliances<br>1. Militant collective action<br>2. Transformationist<br>3. Ends *not* means morally important<br>4. Positive discrimination to promote equal opportunities for minority ethnic groups |
| **General characteristics** | 1. More moderate in relation to the extent and means of change<br>2. Emphasis on the individual learner, and attitudes<br>3. Relativist epistemology<br><br>*New multiculturalism*<br>1. Incorporates explicit antiracist teaching in the curriculum<br>2. Includes emphasis on institutional racism – the need for institutional change | 1. More militant in relation to the extent and means of change<br>2. Emphasis on social groups and institutional structures<br>3. Absolutist (fundamentalist) epistemology<br><br>*Developed antiracism*<br>1. More explicit attention to the curriculum – to antiracist teaching<br>2. More substantive guidance about strategies for social change |

*Social utility*, the fourth value position they describe, is associated with the post-war Welfare State and such values as citizens' rights, equality, participation and social (not simply economic) usefulness. This perspective accepts that the state has responsibility for supporting a higher education from which no individual is excluded through inability to pay.

Becher and Kogan take professional and management values to be about the governance of higher education, and market values and welfarism to be about objectives and ultimate outcomes. They see all four as contending and co-existing forces which will continue to live together 'in different mixes in different institutions and for different functions'.

Although management and market values have become stronger forces in recent times, antiracist higher education would, I suggest, involve a *reversal* of this trend. Professional values with a collegiate approach should be the keynote of university governance, albeit (as we move to a wider participation in higher education) benefiting from good management at central, institutional and basic unit levels, subject to an accountability to a pluralist academic community. Social utility should guide ultimate aims and outcomes.

To put this in terms of the alternative paradigms discussed in the previous chapter, the university of market forces would be governed by management values for market-led results and the traditional university by professional values for elitist ends. The mature and antiracist university would be governed by professional values – where these are those of a pluralist and democratic academy – for the well-being of the wider society of which the university is a part.

Unchecked, market forces would reduce utility to economic considerations and damage good teaching and research. Because not all worthwhile academic activity can be justified in utilitarian terms, higher education, with considerable academic autonomy, deserves society's support. Within this, in lean times, a degree of entrepreneurial activity and funding self-help need not damage what should be a fundamentally *academic and democratic* core.

# 10 | Higher Education for All

Just as *Race for a Change* encapsulates several key themes of the book overall, so the title of this final chapter compresses the main characteristics of its vision of a lifelong, antiracist higher education. 'Higher education for all' echoes the Swann Report's 'Education for all' to similarly emphasize that antiracist higher education is about *mainstream* provision for *all* students, and not just about provision for minority ethnic groups. It also suggests a mass higher education (that is, an expanded and diverse system) in contrast to the current system which provides 'higher education for few'. Finally, 'for all' has a democratic sense, signifying that such a higher education would be in the interests of all social groups.

In what follows, examples are provided of current good practice, drawn from a recent survey into antiracist higher education. In contrasting the current partial realization of antiracism, which the survey revealed, with what could be, I hope that an alternative vision of an antiracist and mature university may be glimpsed.

## HE Ltd: A patchwork of good practice

In February 1991, the history, politics, continuing education, education, sociology, biology and mathematics departments in all British universities were sent a questionnaire (see Appendix 3) which sought information about antiracist education. The questionnaire had two parts: part A sought information about departmental organization and part B information about curriculum development. Its 'yes/no' format was designed to allow computer analysis but with space to provide descriptions of specific policy and practice. One hundred and twenty responses were received, and these provide an indicative general picture of antiracist development across universities, a basis for departmental comparisons – including a comparison with the earlier survey of departments of continuing education – and description of organizational and curriculum practices. Those departments which described practices which seemed to us worth wider dissemination were engaged in telephone interviews about this work and a small number were subsequently visited by one of the researchers. Thus the investigation into good practice was progressively focused.

This research into antiracist practices in higher education was based on a number of key assumptions: that HE departments should develop organizational structures to eliminate racial discrimination; that a genuine 'higher education' will provide a non-ethnocentric and pluralist curriculum; and that it is worthwhile to identify current practices conducive to achieving such an antiracist organization and curriculum in order to disseminate these to other well-intentioned academics. The research was thus change-oriented in that it was always intended that those good practices identified would be disseminated to facilitate and encourage their wider adoption. What follows summarizes and analyses the responses, the telephone interviews and visits, and offers relevant antiracist recommendations to those in higher education.

Departmental responses indicate that thirty-five universities have a written antiracist policy statement. Only seven of the 120 departments to respond reported having their own antiracist policy. This small number recorded more than average activity in response to the remaining questions, supporting the assumption that constructing such policies is an educative process and that adopting a written policy statement can be a trigger for antiracist change.

There were far more positive than negative responses to questions about staff recruitment. However, the closer a candidate comes to being appointed, the less action there is to eliminate discrimination. Thus ninety departments build an antiracist dimension into their job descriptions, eighty-eight into their shortlistings and eighty-six into their interviewing procedures. Very few departments (six) have developed an antiracist staff development programme. Clearly, this represents a huge developmental gap. This finding supports the widely shared view that, however little or however inadequate (Eggleston *et al.* 1986), much more racism awareness education has been received by school than by post-school teachers.

It was encouraging to discover that 89 per cent of departments have recruited students via access courses. This testifies to the (albeit small-scale) success of the access movement. One in three departments have taken other steps to recruit more black students, though few monitor their numbers. One in four departments have made special provision for minority ethnic group students (the details provided suggest this is mainly in the form of English language support). One in four have engaged in relevant action-oriented research, but only seven departments monitor their antiracist development overall.

As one would expect, more departments provide specific courses or units about race relations than claim to have permeated their programme with an antiracist perspective. Nevertheless, a surprisingly large number of departments do make such a claim. Similarly, many deny that their resources are ethnocentric, although twenty-three failed to answer the question and there were some who queried what it meant. Only two departments have tried to recruit black staff, although twenty-three make use of black visiting speakers.

## Identifying good practice

In this section, details are given of practices described by respondents which are conducive to eliminating negative racial discrimination in organizational structures and through curriculum bias.

Several respondents drew a distinction between positive discrimination, which they regard as ethically dubious ('unfair practice'), and positive action, which they saw as legitimate. To some extent, there is a degree of confusion about these terms. It matters less what we call good practice than that we eliminate racism, but the term positive action does seem to convey the intention to fairness more clearly and is thus (wherever appropriate) to be preferred. The point is that positive action refers to those practices adopted to counter or eliminate discrimination in order to *equalize* individual opportunity. Such action to eliminate discrimination may be distinguished from social engineering for proportionate *group* outcomes (as may be required in meeting quotas, for example) and it is this which tends to be referred to as 'positive discrimination'. In my own view, argued more fully elsewhere (Leicester and Lovell 1992), even quotas may be legitimate in some circumstances, particularly since positive discrimination currently happens in the reverse, through unconscious bias. It would certainly seem legitimate to recognize the value in itself of a more ethnically diverse academic staff and thus, other things being equal, of choosing a black candidate in preference to a white one.

Eight descriptions of specific staff recruitment good practices were provided:

1. The advertisement for the post quotes the department's equal opportunities policy. This sends positive signals to potential applicants and thus may tend to increase the number of black applications.
2. Very careful attention is given to applications from black candidates.
3. Positive action in shortlisting.

4. Specifying and recording the reasons for rejecting *all* candidates. This eliminates overt racism and may bring to light implicit or indirect racially biased criteria and assumptions.

5. Having at least one black person and one woman on the panel. It can be less daunting for a black or female interviewee to face a panel that is not all white or all male. Moreover, their presence on the panel will tend to inhibit overt racism and sexism during the panel's decision-making. (In departments which have several black members, those members could choose their representative. Whites *choosing* black representation or men *choosing* female representation is not good antiracist or anti-sexist practice.)

6. Asking all candidates the same range of questions. This is an instance of how good interview practice tends, simultaneously, to be antiracist.

7. The criteria for selection are formalized before the interviews. The interview panel will thus have a shared understanding of the skills required for the job in question. Again this is both good interview practice and will tend to eliminate unnecessary and indirectly racist criteria. When the criteria are not formalized, panels are more likely to appoint 'people like us' – people they find congenial rather than the candidate who can best undertake the tasks required (an ability to promote equal opportunities could be included among the formalized requirements).

8. Specific training in antiracist interviewing and in dealing with racial and sexual harassment had been given to staff in a small number of departments. (Those departments responsible for the training of social workers had also provided courses that placed social work in the context of a multiracial and racist society.)

A number of departments ensure that they publicize their courses in multiracial areas, in multiracial schools and internationally. This attention to ensuring that information reaches black communities includes visits to multiracial schools and community colleges, producing posters in Indian languages, brochure material which incorporates photographs of black students and staff, and distributing this to community centres.

Several departments claimed that their general provision of courses for all students has an antiracist and pluralist perspective. A number specified that all their professional courses incorporate this. Liverpool University's Department of Sociology and Social Work, for example, incorporates race relations in all of its courses. Several departments of education provide courses on antiracist/multicultural education. Some departments offer courses and other forms of support in English language and essay skills for minority ethnic group students, and one department mentioned its pastoral support system as including an adviser for mature students.

Fifteen departments provided details of action research and community development with which they are involved. In a small number of cases, their project included collaboration between members of the department and some other organization. For instance, Oxford's Department of Continuing Education and the Workers' Education Association (WEA) have conducted joint research on returning to learning. Loughborough's Department of English and Drama has worked on devising and producing a play with the local Asian community and plan further such community development initiatives. Individual academics also contribute to regional antiracist developments, and publish relevant books. For example, one department mentioned a book about social work and ethnicity; another academic writes about the history of the Jewish community in Britain; and other individual research projects have focused on race relations in the USA and the Caribbean. In one department (Brunel, Education), the students on various youth and community work training courses regularly undertake action research and community education projects as part of their fieldwork.

Although only seven departments reported any monitoring of their antiracism, those that did described useful practice that others could emulate. Some departments include questions to find out about continuing racial bias and effective positive action in a feedback questionnaire to students at the end of their courses. Others attempt departmental assessment of this as part of their annual review. Some departments include monitoring in the brief of their equal opportunities committee and one department has a special monitoring sub-group.

Thirty-two departments provided 'further details' of their curriculum. About half of these offer specific courses on race and racism. Several history departments include the history and roots of racism in their syllabus. One university history department, in its response to us, set out its academic position which, despite its own perception to the contrary, we see as an instance of good practice:

> As professional historians, all members of this department are engaged in teaching pupils to examine sources and secondary works critically and to be aware of the assumptions built into them. A number of us engage directly with one of the most contentious of all fields of historical study, the history of the European Empires. In doing so, we undoubtedly alert students to problems of bias, not least that of ethnocentricity, and to the difficulties of perception and interpretation which follow. Ethnocentric and (much more rarely) overtly racist writings represent only particular (even if acute) forms of a general problem addressed by all professional historians and their pupils. Naturally we may also choose materials for reading and study which will make pupils aware of the diversity of cultures, of the

achievements of non-European societies, and of oppressive systems such as slavery and apartheid. However, your questionnaire seems to imply that we should go much further, for example, in their 'positive' criticism and selection of teaching materials. Our own position is rather the much carefully studied one, conveniently set out in the recent Final Report of the National Curriculum History Working Group (copy of relevant para. 11.26 enclosed). From our reading and our selection of materials we may hope or assume that students will develop certain kinds of awareness, mental habits, and a sense of the values of tolerance, respect and so on. However, they may not do so, and if they either choose not to do so or simply draw their own different conclusions, that is their right. 'Positive' discrimination and selection to the point of indoctrination, and 'positive' antiracist teaching, only undermine the integrity of history teaching, however worthy the cause.

Some departments of politics include Third World politics and apartheid. One education department described their provision as patchy with a small number of their courses incorporating multicultural education. However, another department (Glasgow, Sociology) claimed that shared awareness across the staff ensures good permeation across all courses, and yet another (York, Sociology) has a policy of incorporating equal opportunities issues into all of its courses.

On the whole, maths and science departments have paid least attention to developing a multicultural curriculum. A small number felt that this discipline was inherently 'universal':

> I believe some of your questions are not relevant for teaching university mathematics . . . I strongly object to your slanted (Q12), suggesting that unless we advertise our courses via the CRC (say), black people won't learn of our existence. This is a slur, both on black people and on us. Similarly, what would be the point of putting out information leaflets in 'other languages'? We are desperately short of cash, we want to get qualified students, but to imagine it a rational act to translate our course information into Gujerati and bombard the CRC with leaflets strains credibility.

Not all mathematics departments shared this view.

> One cannot say that there is general awareness, in staff or students generally, of the relevance of importance of an understanding of racism and its roots, and of a non-eurocentric perspective, in a subject such as Mathematics.

> Mathematics, of all subjects, appears to most people as 'objective', 'value-free', and as free from even the possibility of cultural bias.

A great deal needs to be done to make teachers *at all levels* aware of how cultural influences do permeate the teaching of mathematics. I know of some good work in this area which was carried out under ILEA (now abolished), and magazines such as *Race and Class* do sometimes address this question.

On the issue of racism in education generally, there have been good developments; but on the whole the pressures which black people face (which start as early as nursery school level with name-calling, etc.) are greatly underestimated by the white majority.

What I feel is needed, at university level and elsewhere, is a *real commitment* to listen to black people, to understand their needs and to act, rather than to posture with superficial statements, etc.

The University of Hull is, I believe, moving in the right direction.

Twenty-one telephone interviews and four visits confirmed much of the information gained from the questionnaires (Leicester and Lovell 1991). The researchers found some interviewees became defensive when asked about race issues, seeming most comfortable when responding to questions about access and admissions. Some additional examples of good practice emerged, particularly in relation to professional courses. One interviewee responsible for in-service courses for teachers described how she asks the teachers to bring in the textbooks they commonly use in school and these are analysed against four published checklists for race and gender bias. I do something similar with MEd students in continuing education who bring in the materials they use with their own adult students. I usually divide the group into smaller units and first ask them to construct their own antiracist checklist and then use this to evaluate, in their group, the resources they use.

This research into antiracist practice in higher education was dependent on what was reported to us by individuals. We recognize that there might be some tendency to present one's own department in the best possible light. Nevertheless, there was a consistency in the findings across departments and in those emerging from questionnaires, telephone interviews and visits. For example, we consistently found more initiatives in relation to recruitment practice than staff development.

The response rate was good. Only two departments said they were not prepared to answer a questionnaire that was not anonymous. Only one respondent perceived our research to be itself racist, because it was based on ideas of positive discrimination, and two mathematics departments perceived the curricular questions to be irrelevant to their discipline. A slightly more widespread failure to understand the term 'ethnocentric' and the notion of 'permeating the curriculum with an antiracist perspective' reveal a lack of familiarity with the idea of an anti-racist education.

The most important general finding, as with the earlier UCACE surveys of CE departments, was that good practice in higher education is patchy. It arises mostly from the commitment of individuals, not from departmental policy. We thus have a picture of very limited developments which have not been built into structures and routines. In other words, although we found creditable instances of antiracism, these cannot be said to be characteristic.

## Summary and synthesis

At this point, a synopsis of the preceding material will give some indication of the key points. The issues explored and the contentions made in separate chapters not only interrelate but do so in mutually supportive ways to form a consistent account of antiracist continuing and higher education.

Conceptual analysis revealed that the concept of racism is many-stranded. One strand involves the notion of power-backed prejudice, another that of (often unwitting) institutional discrimination. Prejudice is learned. Hence the importance given to the antiracist transformation of an individual's meaning perspective through continuing education, and to the continuing of an antiracist curriculum across the whole of higher education. And, since institutional discrimination perpetuates racial disadvantage, there was an emphasis on continuing education through anti-oppressive social action and on ways of changing discriminatory university organizational and decision-making procedures.

These various conceptions of racism were found to be embedded in the idea of justice. Practices count as racially unjust (racist) in so far as they result in black groups receiving disproportionately less of the good things (HE places, educational qualifications, promotion, etc.) and disproportionately more of the bad things (unemployment, poor housing, etc.). Inequality of access to good things is manifested in various and sometimes indirect ways. We see here the connection between antiracist education and the movement towards equal opportunities in education, and the relation of these to the kinds of positive action advocated in this book.

Attention was also given to the longstanding and influential debate about whether education should be multicultural or antiracist. I argue that these two conceptions of education, although distinguishable, over-lap. Moreover, it makes political sense, in the present conservative climate, for proponents of each model of education to be allies. Again the basis for transformation is *both* individual learning, through a pluralist and antiracist curriculum and pedagogy, *and* institutional structures through democratizing, antiracist change.

There has been a more esoteric debate on cultural relativism arising from the idea of a multicultural curriculum. Are there culture-transcendent elements (conceptions, rational principles, values) by which such a curriculum could be constructed? I would argue that there is some degree of cultural specificity such that a multicultural education will require an individual's initiation into a variety of cultural perspectives (to enable wider synthesizing possibilities in developing individual meaning perspectives) and the enrichment of our collective understandings through ongoing cross-cultural dialogue. This view is consistent with the constructivist epistemology underpinning this book. These epistemological considerations support my contention that a monocultural, ethnocentric education in our universities will impoverish higher education in its central task – the pursuit and dissemination of knowledge.

Antiracist education was placed in historical context, including consideration of the likely impact of recent education 'reform' acts (see notes to Chapter 4). I argue that antiracist continuing education is a lifelong matter with implications at all levels and for all stages of education. In discussing 'good teaching', the distinction between androgogy and pedagogy was questioned. Well-grounded androgogical assumptions apply to children as well as to adults. While not denying that adult experience is more extensive, good teaching in all sections will respect the learner, make use of her or his previous experience and of experiential methodology.

In Chapter 3, the concept of 'antiracist continuing education' was considered in the light of influential ideas in this field. Antiracist continuing education was seen as involving the antiracist transformation of individual learning through engaging in relevant social action. This conception of continuing education is consistent with my concept of higher education. Higher education is seen as a second-order pursuit of knowledge and understanding. Thus academics in university continuing education will seek to analyse and understand the first-order process of empowerment education outlined above. An individual's 'meaning perspective' will draw on, and may contribute to, the collective understandings which constitute objective knowledge.

In addition to this analysis of the concept of antiracist continuing education, attention has been given to the thing itself. What is antiracist continuing education in practical terms and how can departments appropriately develop their current work? A UCACE-related survey provided an overall picture of what departments are currently doing about ethnicity and education, and some principles of good practice emerged. Similar principles were also found in the description and discussion of my more general survey of other departments in HE institutions.

The ethos of a department may be more or less conducive to antiracist development. Less democratic organizational structures and decision making allow little more than tokenistic changes motivated by individual academics. Triggers to action at departmental level include staff development, the construction of a departmental policy and the creation of an equal opportunities committee and/or monitoring group. Taking steps to increase black staff is important, as is action to institutionalize antiracist developments so that they become built into departmental routine.

The important post-school issue of access was included. What can be done to encourage greater participation in higher education by minority ethnic groups? The discussion included consideration of courses and other devices to facilitate entry and also the wider issue of rendering the institution congenial to a more diverse clientele.

From the outset, I suggested that departments of continuing education are agents of change within their own university. They have traditions, values, experience (and in some cases an official brief) relevant to such a role. Inreach activity across the university can bring progressive developments into the mainstream of higher education. Outreach work with local communities can act as a bridge or link to minority ethnic group organizations, individuals and perspectives. The UCACE survey illustrates that many departments have accepted a change agent role with some success and are engaging in this inreach and outreach work. Academics in CE departments thus have two activist tasks, departmental and institutional; that is, antiracist development of their own department (antiracist continuing education) and of their institution (continuing antiracist education into higher education).

In Part 2, the centre of attention shifted from university continuing education to higher education *per se*. An analysis of 'higher education' as the pursuit of intrinsically worthwhile second-order knowledge and understanding places emphasis on research and teaching as *the* central HE tasks. Research is the means by which objective knowledge (shared understandings, collective meaning perspectives) is constructed. Teaching facilitates the individual student's initiation into this shared realm.

Because knowledge is a product of human endeavour and is related to group as well as universal interests, it is vital that all social groups have a part in that collective task. It is crucial that diversity of experience enriches our shared understanding and that minority voices are not drowned out. Just as Carol Gilligan's attention to women's stories enlarged our understanding of moral development, so HE research will be enriched in so far as we find ways of hearing the full range of narratives. Part of the way to achieve this is to establish a less elitist and more diverse community of scholars. The central tasks of higher education are potentially better done, not worse, if wider access is achieved. (I believe these epistemological claims to be deeply important but easily misunderstood.)

It should be mentioned here that other things, some of which are currently in danger, also influence the quality of higher education. Quality requires adequate resourcing, to allow effective teacher/student ratios for example, and research that is not over-dependent on partisan funders. A worthwhile higher education cannot be the product of market forces alone.

All of the chapters in this book are based on the belief that continuing and higher education should be antiracist. Justice, as a fundamental value, is the justification for this and for the book as a whole. Within it, subsidiary justifications are given in the form of analysis intended to support particular conceptions of continuing and higher education. There are *also* these subsidiary epistemological considerations suggesting that a pluralistic higher education would be more effective in relation to the pursuit of knowledge (these are not meant to *replace* the value-based justification that it ought, in justice, to be pluralistic). I also seek to indicate what an antiracist education might be like at this level. The empirical surveys produced examples of good practice. In this context, 'good practice' was understood in terms of activities with the capacity to promote racial justice in education. Thus I would contend that the underpinning values, epistemological considerations and descriptions of, and prescriptions for, good practice are coherent across chapters and mutually supportive.

At the outset, two claims were made: that antiracism would transform continuing and higher education and that departments of continuing education could be change agents in the task of transforming higher education. As I have said, the UCACE survey provides some empirical support for this claim of change agent capacity, since there is evidence that some departments are already, and with some success, undertaking such a role. Clearly, there is much more to be done, including the logically prior task of transforming continuing education.

The HE questionnaire indicates that many other departments are at much the same stage as the more progressive CE departments and so may themselves have useful experiences to share. In what follows, I have tried to bring together these scattered instances of antiracist higher education into a more integrated picture.

## Higher education transformed

This is no time to engage in the luxury of cooling off or to take the tranquilizing drug of gradualism. Now is the time to make real the promises of democracy; now is the time to rise from the dark and desolate valley of segregation to the sunlit path of racial justice . . . I say to you today, my friends, even though we face the difficulties of today and tomorrow, I still have a dream. It is a dream deeply rooted in the American dream. I have a dream that one day this nation will rise up and live out the true meaning of its creed, 'We hold these truths to be self evident, that all men are created equal'.

(Martin Luther King Jr, 28 August 1963)

When teaching on racism and education, I often make use of experiential exercises from the Katz handbook on antiracist training (Katz 1978). One exercise in particular effectively shows students how extensively racism permeates our institutions, and some concrete antiracist goals are produced. First, we brainstorm for about five minutes on the aspects that together constitute a university (or college, or school, or hospital, etc.). The blackboard is soon covered with the students' suggestions: teaching and ancillary staff, students, curriculum, books, other learning resources, buildings, committees, funding, and so on. The students then divide into three groups. One group is asked to design a deliberately racist university; another to design an unintentionally racist university; and the third to design an antiracist university. About forty-five minutes later, each subgroup reports back. It has always been the case that the deliberately racist group present a picture of deliberate apartheid and that the unintentionally racist group's university is soon perceived to be a description of the current *status quo*: monolingual, mainly white, all white at the top, hierarchical, and so on. The third group provide the blueprint for change as they describe a multilingual, multiracial, democratic and pluralist institution. There are proportionate numbers of black people at all levels of the system, the books and other learning resources are pluralist, the very posters on the walls are in several languages with illustrations that depict a multiracial society, etc. We then discuss strategies for moving from university two to university three.

This is to discuss piecemeal and cumulative change, since discussion tends to focus on achievable changes that individuals and small groups can initiate (one does what one can because that is all one can do). As individual academics, we can seek to promote equal opportunities for individuals, for example, through better access which discriminates less on irrelevant grounds of race, class or gender. We can develop our own curriculum in antiracist and pluralist ways. This is a liberal approach to change – seeking gradual, partial improvement. Better access to an unchanged institution is a progressive though partial gain. Antiracist curriculum development of competitive degree courses is a progressive though partial development.

A more radical approach to change would require positive discrimination towards equality for currently less privileged social groups. It would need a fundamental transformation, rather than a cumulative improvement of what we now have. Such a transformation would involve change on *all* fronts; open access to well-resourced and non-competitive, antiracist, flexible, pluralist provision of modules which do not primarily seek to credentialize individuals, but to empower them to promote democracy and justice. In this utopian university, no student with the capacity to benefit from higher education would be excluded and all would feel at home there. The decision-making processes would not be hidden and each decision would be made by all those who would be affected by it. This commitment to equality would also influence interpersonal relations and, feeling secure as never before, people would be collaborative and not competitive, as befits the essentially social tasks of pursuing and transmitting knowledge. (Contrast this with the actual situation: for example, the differences in conditions of employment and status between academics and ancillary staff, between academics and 'their' research assistants, and between staff and students, all in an intensely competitive milieu.)

Realistically, such a utopian revolution is, to say the least, extremely unlikely, but aiming for it we may maximize the degree of *antiracist maturity* which our universities actually achieve. Dreams sometimes bring their own realization just a little nearer . . .

I will therefore end with this dream of *higher education for all*, in which the ideal university is an antiracist academy which includes all voices in its ongoing debates. Here black and white colleagues, women and men with a diversity of experience, cultural background and perspective, collaborate as equals in the collective tasks of constructing and disseminating worthwhile knowledge.

# Appendix 1
# Resources to Support Antiracist Work in Post-16 Education

## General

African Caribbean Community Development Unit
*African, Caribbean and Asian Trainers' Directory*
ACCDU, London, 1991
ISBN 0 901171 98 0
A list of over 70 black trainers from all over the UK (though with a preponderance of London-based trainers). A wide range of training areas is covered, including: race and gender issues, management, staffing, equal opportunities, mental health, community work and economic development.
Available from London Voluntary Services Council.
Price £3.50 (voluntary organizations)/£6.80 (statutory organizations).

Ball, Wendy
*Post-sixteen Education and the Promotion of Equal Opportunities: A Case Study of Policies and Provision in One Local Authority* (Policy Papers in Ethnic Relations, No. 8)
Centre for Research in Ethnic Relations, Coventry, 1987
An account of the approach taken by a West Midlands local authority towards promoting equal opportunities in post-16 education. The institutions covered include: a community college, a college of further education, a polytechnic, a college of adult education, the careers service, and community-based education provision. This study is especially useful because the borough was in the course of restructuring its post-16 education, in order to introduce a comprehensive integrated system of tertiary education. This pointed up contrasts between the stages reached by different institutions in developing equal opportunities policies, between the way that policies were introduced (e.g. 'top down' or 'bottom up' approaches) and between the strategies they have adopted. At the time of the study, the college of adult education was the only part of the proposed tertiary system that had not even started to consider equal opportunities *vis-à-vis* black people and women.

Dadzie, Stella
*Educational Guidance with Black Communities: A Checklist of Good Practice*
National Institute of Adult Continuing Education, Leicester, 1990

A publication giving help to anyone involved in educational guidance who wants to examine their own practice and ensure that their guidance service is establishing and developing antiracist ways of working. The checklists, covering aspects of work from informing and advising to staff development, enable staff to set themselves clear objectives for bringing about change in their service. The checklists were developed as a result of a REPLAN-FATEBU (Forum for the Advancement of Training and Education for the Black Unemployed) conference.

Eggleston, S.J. *et al.*
*Education for Some: The Educational and Vocational Experiences of 15–18 Year Old Young People of Ethnic Minority Groups*
Trentham Books, Stoke-on-Trent, 1986
ISBN 0 948080 06 X
Report of a research report which examined the educational achievements, the educational and vocational aspirations and the employment of young black people. It looks at their schools, the careers service, destinations/examinations at 16+, young people in continuing education and in the labour market, and schemes for unemployed school leavers. It makes recommendations to schools, further education, the careers service, LEAs, the DFE and the DoE for steps they can take to counteract racial discrimination and promote greater equality of opportunity.

Further Education Unit
*Antiracist Strategies in College and Community*
FEU, London, 1989
ISBN 1 85338 150 1
A short pamphlet which summarizes two projects undertaken to help implement Manchester LEA's antiracist policies. The Community Education Service and three colleges of further education collaborated to work on staff and curriculum development. The summary includes a useful checklist for antiracist materials evaluation and some pointers for useful strategies.
Free publication.

Further Education Unit/REPLAN
*Working with Young Adults in a Multicultural Context*
FEU/REPLAN, London, 1987
ISBN 0 948621 95 8
Bulletin summarizing a project aiming to develop curricular strategies designed to make further and higher education more accessible to unemployed (especially African-Caribbean) young adults.
Free publication.

Inner London Education Authority
*Race, Sex and Class, 5: Multi-ethnic Education in Further, Higher and Community Education*
ILEA, London, 1983
A short paper outlining the principles on which ILEA based its provision, describing existing initiatives and good practice, and giving information about guidelines which had been produced for each sector: colleges, polytechnics, adult education institutes and the youth service.

Runnymede Trust
*Education for Some: A Summary of the Eggleston Report on the Educational and Vocational Experiences of Young Black People*
Runnymede Trust, London, 1986
*See* Eggleston *et al.* for details of the full report.

Sammons, Pam and Newbury, Karen
*Ethnic Monitoring in Further and Higher Education: An Account of ILEA's Initiative* (RP 521, Part 1)
FEU, London, 1989
ISBN 1 85338 160 8
A record of ILEA's experience of developing an ethnic monitoring system, and of the part this played in opening up access to further and higher education. There is a list of recommendations and some useful appendices including antiracist policies, notes on practical aspects of data collection and processing, and samples of an enrolment form and an explanatory leaflet for students.
Free publication.

Unit for the Development of Adult Continuing Education
*Black Community Access*
UDACE/NIACE, Leicester, 1990
ISBN 1 872941 00 1
A development paper which focuses on practical ways in which collaboration between black community organizations and institutions of further and higher education can help to improve participation, opportunities and achievement for black adults. It includes seven case studies of collaboration from across the country, covering both college-based initiatives and education projects within the community.

# Continuing/adult education

Cassara, Beverly Benner (Ed.)
*Adult Education in a Multicultural Society*
Routledge, London, 1990
ISBN 0 415 03644 5
An account of the US experience of providing adult education in a multicultural society. The contributors examine the questions raised by pluralism and linguistic diversity, and consider the role of adult education as an agent of social change. The book concentrates on the importance of catering for the needs of minority ethnic groups, giving examples of the adult education provided for some of the larger ethnic groups in the USA. However, there is no consideration of a specifically antiracist perspective and what this might mean for staff development or for an antiracist curriculum for all adult education students.

Further Education Unit
*Black Perspectives on Adult Education: Identifying the Needs* (RP 236)
FEU, London, 1989

ISBN 1 85338 106 3
Report of a project to begin the process of devising and implementing antiracist strategies for curriculum development and related institutional changes in a multiracial adult education service. It includes a review of current provision, an examination of selected areas of the curriculum, and a consideration of staff development and support needs.
Free publication.

Gordon, Paul *et al.*
*Antiracist Resources: A Guide for Adult and Community Education*
Runnymede Trust, London, 1988
ISBN 0 902397 77 X
A valuable compilation of information about resources with an antiracist perspective, for use by people working in community and adult education. It includes listings of books, magazines, films and videos, posters, performers and organizations. The materials included are intended to be useful both for teaching *about* issues of race, and for integrating an antiracist perspective into the work of community and adult educators.

*Multicultural Teaching*, 6(1): Winter 1987
Special issue on continuing education
Trentham Books, Stoke-on-Trent, 1987
A collection of articles on race issues and continuing/adult education.

Open University
*Racism in the Workplace and Community*
Open University, Milton Keynes, 1983
An information pack designed for use in community and trade union education. It looks at topics such as: 'What is racism?', the law, employment and trade unions, and racism and the community. It includes worksheets for use with course members.

Trade Union and Basic Education Project (TUBE)
*Ten Years of Community Education in the Inner City: A Report of Education Work Undertaken by the WEA North Western District's Trade Union and Basic Education Project*
WEA North Western District, Manchester
An account of the work of a project whose specific objective was to engage with the educational needs of ethnic minority and black groups in Manchester. It outlines the various kinds of education provided (health courses, political education, trade union education, basic education) and looks at educational practice. A valuable source of practical ideas, especially for: descriptions of TUBE's methods of making contact, working with community groups and identifying their needs; case studies of particular projects; outlines of courses; a practical evaluation of achievements and shortcomings of the project's work.
Available from WEA North Western District, £3.00 + p&p.

Workers' Educational Association
*The WEA and Black Communities*
WEA, London, 1987
Report of a working party on WEA provision for black communities, which looks particularly at course curricula, community liaison and access, and equal opportunities. The report outlines the findings of two surveys: one of adult education for black communities in WEA districts, the other of the adult education needs of a sample of black community organizations. It goes on to describe the approach of the successful TUBE project in Manchester and then makes recommendations on access, antiracist staff development, district review, funding and equal opportunities.

# Further education

Borthwick, Andrew *et al.*
*Planning NAFE. Equal Opportunities for Ethnic Minorities: A Handbook for Senior LEA and College Managers and Training Agency Officers* (RP 396)
FEU, London, 1988
ISBN 1 85338 097 0
A practical handbook focusing on key areas relating to the provision of equality of opportunity for people from minority ethnic groups in access to non-advanced further education (NAFE). In each of twelve 'Areas for action', a statement of principle is followed by a list of 'indicators of application' (possible sources of evidence that principles are being put into practice) and a checklist.
Free publication.

Early Years Trainers Antiracist Network
*Selecting for Equality*
EYTARN, London, n.d.
A very clear and practical outline of the principles and practices on which the recruitment and selection of students and staff need to be based to achieve equality of opportunity. It gives guidance on advertising, prospectuses and application forms, on the drafting of job descriptions and on interview planning and management. There are useful examples of application forms and of interview questions, guidance notes, criteria lists and report forms. While some of the examples given are specific to the selection of students for 'early years' work, the majority of recommendations are applicable to recruitment procedures generally.
Price £5.00.

Early Years Trainers Antiracist Network
*Training for Equality*
EYTARN, London, n.d.
A collection of activities designed to be used by trainers working with students on childcare or education courses, or for in-service staff development. It focuses on the effects of racism on young children, both black and white, and on ways of developing an antiracist practice to counter this. Individual activities (e.g. on stereotyping, discrimination) are relevant to a range of training programmes.
Price £4.50.

Forum TV
*Worlds Apart* (Video, 30 minutes)
Forum TV, Bristol, 1987
Black people recount their experience of racism in further education, and their struggle to overcome the restrictions which prevent them from gaining access to it. The video also looks at some of the action taking place to try to remove those barriers. Useful as stimulus material. There is an accompanying booklet.
Price £30.00.

Further Education Unit
*Access to Mainstream Further Education for Unemployed Black Adults: Project Information Bulletin* (RP 413/REPLAN)
FEU, London, 1987
Report of a project which aimed to devise and test guidelines for mainstream further education providers who wish to increase opportunities for unemployed black adults.
Free publication.

Further Education Unit
*Access to Vocational FE for Unemployed Black Adults* (RP 413)
FEU, London, n.d.
Report of a project aiming to pilot access to vocational further education for black unemployed people in Liverpool, focusing on three particular subject areas: Health Studies, Electronics and Music Workshop. It makes recommendations on courses, institutional change and curriculum issues, as well as giving guidelines for providers of further education.
Free publication.

Further Education Unit
*Black Perspectives on FE Provision: A Summary Document*
DES, London, 1985
ISBN 0 946469 84 9
A short summary of research carried out at the Open College of South London and Bradford and Ilkley Community College. In London, the researchers sought the views of young African-Caribbean people on what they wanted from post-school education, what the barriers were and what kinds of courses they wanted. The Bradford study surveyed the views of young Asians on FE college provision and looked at the distribution of Asian students in further education and at parental influence over educational choice.
Free publication.

Further Education Unit
*Curriculum Development for a Multicultural Society: Policy and Curriculum. An FEU View*
FEU, London, 1985
ISBN 0 946469 69 5
This report identifies three sets of issues – equal opportunities, the multicultural society and racism – and gives useful checklists for LEAs and colleges in each of

these areas. It goes on to give examples of LEA and college action, including policy statements, ethnic record-keeping, guidance on racist incidents and staff development. There is a summary of findings on black perspectives on FE provision, and some useful appendices, giving facts and figures on the effects of racism in society, and a glossary of terms.

Free publication.

Further Education Unit
*FE in Black and White: Staff Development Needs in a Multicultural Society*
Longman, York, 1987
ISBN 0 582 01876 5
A survey of staff development needs, which formed the basis of the FEU project 'Staff development for a multicultural society' (RP 390). It makes recommendations under the following heads: information and awareness, curriculum change, teaching and learning strategies, and management issues.

Further Education Unit
*Implementing Multicultural and Antiracist Education in Mainly White Colleges*
FEU, London, 1991
ISBN 1 85338 246 9
Report of a project which attempted to explore ways in which colleges with few ethnic minority students might bring about curriculum changes along antiracist lines. It suggests teaching strategies for engaging with issues of racism and gives examples of work carried out with groups of students at Monkwearmoth Colleges of Further Education.

Price £8.00.

Further Education Unit
*Staff Development for a Multicultural Society: A Materials Package* (RP 390)
FEU, London, 1988
ISBN 1 85338 104 7
A package of materials produced to support a national staff development programme in further education: the package consists of five booklets ('Introductory module', 'Institutional change', 'Curriculum change', 'Strategies for mainly white areas' and 'Teaching and learning strategies'), a video to accompany the training and a handbook – *Training the Trainers*.

Copies of the package are available from the FEU, price £63.90.

Further Education Unit
*Working with Adults: Curricular Strategies for a Multicultural Society. Final Report*
FEU, London, n.d.
A report which outlines in a very practical way the development and piloting of curricular strategies in non-advanced further education/training for adult learners, to combat the racist bias inherent in most curricula, books and learning materials. It examines the interaction between institutional structure and curricular strategies, analyses the components necessary to make the strategies effective,

and describes the development of antiracist materials and the staff development undertaken. A 'Practitioners' manual' forms a substantial part of the report and is a valuable source of ideas for others wishing to develop their work in this area. It consists of four sections: (1) an outline of a staff development workshop on revision and development of materials; (2) approaches to developing an understanding of contemporary Britain for all students; (3) approaches to developing skills in written expression for all students; and (4) resources. Because of its typewritten, spiral-bound format, this document is both bulky and difficult to find one's way around. However, it contains much useful material that is not available elsewhere.
Free publication.

Shukla, Krishna and National Antiracist Movement in Education Team
*Mainstream Curricula in a Multicultural Society* (RP 317)
FEU, London, 1989
ISBN 1 85338 155 1
Report of a project which examined the curriculum in three subject areas: Catering, Construction, and Hairdressing and Beauty Care. It looks at the inclusion/ omission of a black perspective, the number of black students on courses, the ethos of FE colleges, national syllabuses and other documents from examining bodies, and staff and student perspectives. There is a list of recommendations to examining/validating bodies, LEAs, the DFE and the DoE on: antiracist policies; involvement of black communities; staff development; monitoring; and the employment of black staff within examination boards, further education and LEAs.
Free publication.

# Higher education

Brandt, Godfrey, *et al.*
*Black Students and Access to Higher Education: Summary of a Feasibility Study*
FEU, London, 1987
An investigation of the quality of the experience of black students in higher education, and of the interface between further and higher education in the provision of Access opportunities for black students. It surveys the policies of HE institutions on access, access routes, courses chosen by Access students and criteria for entry. It includes recommendations on curriculum issues, support for students and staff development.
Free publication.

Committee of Vice-Chancellors and Principals
*Equal Opportunities in Employment in Universities*
CVCP, London, 1991
A document giving general guidance on good practice in equal opportunities, followed by a consideration of issues specific to the employment of ethnic minorities, women and people with disabilities.

Committee of Vice-Chancellors and Principals
*Sexual and Racial Harassment: Guidance for Universities*
CVCP, London, 1990
Guidelines on adopting and implementing a policy statement on harassment, along with guidelines for university staff and students.

Williams, Jenny *et al.*
*Words or Deeds? A Review of Equal Opportunity Policies in Higher Education*
Commission for Racial Equality, London, 1989
ISBN 1 85442 001 1
A 'snapshot' of the development and nature of equal opportunities policies in higher education in the mid-1980s, resulting from a questionnaire sent out to all universities and polytechnics. It gives a summary of findings, followed by an outline of the stages that a university/polytechnic might go through in the course of setting up and implementing an equal opportunities policy. It concludes that universities and polytechnics have been relatively untouched by the debate on racial equality in education and that they have not seen the need to develop policies. It notes that the situation may be changing following the CRE's investigation of medical school admissions.

## List of publishers

Centre for Research on Ethnic Relations
Arts Building
University of Warwick
Coventry CV4 7AL
Tel: 0203 523523

Commission for Racial Equality
Elliot House
10–12 Allington Street
London SW1 5EH
Tel: 071 828 7022

Committee of Vice-Chancellors and Principals
29 Tavistock Square
London WC1 9EZ
Tel: 071 387 9231

Early Years Trainers Anti-Racist Network
1 The Lyndens
51 Granville Road
London N12 0JH
Tel: 081 446 7056

Forum TV
11 Regent Street
Clifton
Bristol BS8 4HW
Tel: 0272 741490

Further Education Unit
Information Centre
Citadel Place
Tinworth Street
London SE11 5EH
Tel: 071 962 1280

London Voluntary Services Council
68 Charlton Street
London NW1 1JR
Tel: 071 388 0241

National Institute of Adult Continuing Education
19B De Montfort Street
Leicester LE1 7GE
Tel: 0533 551451

Open University
LMSO
PO Box 188
Open University
Milton Keynes MK7 6AA
Tel: 0908 274066

Routledge
11 New Fetter Lane
London EC4P 4EE
Tel: 071 583 9855

Runnymede Trust
11 Princelet Street
London E1 6QH
Tel: 071 375 1496

Trentham Books
13–14 Trent Trading Park
Botteslow Street
Stoke-on-Trent ST1 3LY
Tel: 0782 274227

Unit for the Development of Adult Continuing Education
94B London Road
Leicester LE2 0QS
Tel: 0533 542645

Workers' Educational Association
9 Upper Berkeley Street
London W1H 8BY
Tel: 071 402 5608

Workers' Educational Association
North Western District
4th Floor, Crawford House
Precinct Centre
Oxford Road
Manchester M13 9GH
Tel: 061 273 7652

# Appendix 2
# UCACE Recommendations

1. That University Departments of Continuing Education should take the lead within their institutions in the formulation and adoption of equal opportunities and antiracism policy statements at Departmental, Faculty and University level.

2. That University Departments of Continuing Education should use examples of good practice in curriculum developments both to modify their own curriculum and to encourage their institutions to review curriculum design and content across the faculties.

3. That university job descriptions, and recruitment and appointing procedures should embody practices which ensure equality of opportunity; and that this requires recruitment procedures which encourage applications from groups which are currently underrepresented within the staff of the institution, and selection procedures which identify candidates with appropriate knowledge and experience to develop a socially and culturally diverse curriculum.

4. That staff development programmes involving all levels of staff should be implemented which combine training in the awareness of race issues with discussion and information on how specific institutional changes can be brought about.

5. That within the current expansion of access course provision attention should be paid by University Departments of Continuing Education to the need both for access courses targeted specifically at black students and for there to be an increase in the numbers of black students on general access courses.

6. That Universities should develop their curricula to take account of the perspectives and interests of the increasing numbers of black students progressing from access courses to degree level study – both standard age and mature students.

7. That Universities should develop appropriate means of student support and counselling for 'non-traditional' students, including black students.

8. That University CPE providers should consider whether provision focused specifically on the needs and situations of particular black professionals should be made.

9. That University CPE providers should consult with the appropriate professional

bodies to develop training strategies to increase the numbers of black people coming into the professions.

10. That examples of good practice in action-research community education for black people should be used by Departments of Continuing Education to develop a community education strand to their provision for the minority ethnic communities.

11. That both Departments of Continuing Education and Universities as a whole should develop appropriate ethnic monitoring procedures within the context of an equal opportunities policy.

12. That the attention of University decision-makers be drawn to the UFC's commitment to provide higher payment per FTE for work with the 'disadvantaged' (including work with black people) than for the 'normal' continuing education provision and should note that institutions may well benefit financially from developing a strand of such work in future.

13. That, equally, Universities and Departments of Continuing Education should bear in mind that a substantial amount of development in minority ethnic education with Universities can be accomplished without additional financial resources being made available.

# Appendix 3
# Antiracist Higher Education Questionnaire

Name: _____

University: _____

Department: _____

Notes

1. Please mark with a tick (✓) the appropriate answer.

2. 'Black' primarily denotes African-Caribbean and Asian home students, the relevant questions are mainly concerned with those minority ethnic groups who most experience racial discrimination.

3. We are concerned in this questionnaire with antiracist higher education whether developed through antiracist policies or as part of equal opportunities policy development.

## PART A

1. Does your university have a written antiracist statement?

Yes ☐
No ☐

2. Does your university have an equal opportunities policy statement?

Yes ☐
No ☐

3. Does your department have its own written antiracist and/or equal opportunity policy statement?

Yes ☐
No ☐

If you answered YES, please could you enclose a copy.

4. Does your department adopt any equal opportunities/antiracist practices in relation to:

    (i) Job descriptions                                                     Yes ☐
                                                            No ☐

    (ii) Advertising posts                                                  Yes ☐
                                                            No ☐

    (iii) Shortlisting                                                    Yes ☐
                                                          No ☐

    (iv) Interviewing                                                    Yes ☐
                                                          No ☐

If YES to any of the above, please describe the practices.

5. Has your department had staff development programmes about antiracist education as part of equal opportunities or antiracist policy?

                                                          Yes ☐
                                                          No ☐

If YES please send any documentation or other details.

6. Does your department plan to have staff development programmes about antiracist education as part of equal opportunities or antiracist policy?

                                                          Yes ☐
                                                          No ☐

7. Are there students from Access Courses (open entry programmes which replace A Levels but take students, often mature students, to the equivalent standard) within your department?

                                                          Yes ☐
                                                          No ☐

8. Has your department taken any steps to increase the number of black students coming into your courses?

                                                          Yes ☐
                                                          No ☐

If YES to any of the above, please describe the practices.

9. Does your department make any special provision for these groups of students? For example, Access courses targeted at minority groups, relevant extramural certificated courses, community languages, African/Caribbean/Asian studies, components on race relations within professional courses.

Yes ☐
No ☐

If YES, please give brief details.

10. Has your department engaged in any action research or community development education connected with race relations?

Yes ☐
No ☐

If YES, please describe.

11. (i) Do you elicit ethnic background on staff application forms?

Yes ☐
No ☐

(ii) Do you also keep written records obtained by students indicating their ethnic group?

Yes ☐
No ☐

(iii) Do you monitor antiracist practice in your department? For example, evaluation of antiracist curriculum development as part of course assessment: evaluation of recruitment procedures.

Yes ☐
No ☐

If YES, please indicate these evaluative methods.

12. Does your department make information concerning courses accessible for black people? For example, information in 'other' languages, liaison with local CRC and community organizations, use of black people in brochure photographs etc.

Yes ☐
No ☐

If YES, please give any relevant details.

## PART B (CURRICULUM)

13. Are there modules or a unit on race or race relations in the courses offered within the department?

Yes ☐
No ☐

If YES, please give brief details or attach documentation if available.

14. Does an antiracist perspective permeate the department's teaching? For example, does the syllabus take account of the roots and forms of racism and other aspects of race relations?

Yes ☐
No ☐

If YES, please give details elaborating on this development.

15. Do you consider that your department's teaching approach includes the following (please tick (✓) where appropriate) within the department?
    (a) Lecture only ☐
    (b) Lectures and discussion groups ☐
    (c) Experiential and participatory sessions ☐

16. Do you consider that your department's reading lists and other learning resources are ethnocentric?

Yes ☐

No ☐

If NO, please give details of the steps which have been taken to ensure culturally plural and antiracist resources.

17. Do you have a policy statement to recruit black people within your department?

Yes ☐

No ☐

If YES, please give details.

18. Is there a commitment to involve black people in your department, for example black visiting lecturers?

Yes ☐

No ☐

If YES, please give details.

If you wish to add further information or comments on the questionnaire please do so in the space provided below.

Please send completed questionnaires to Tessa Lovell.


THANK YOU FOR YOUR TIME AND COOPERATION

Mal Leicester (Lecturer)
Department of Continuing Education
University of Warwick

Tessa Lovell (Research Assistant)
Department of Continuing Education
University of Warwick

# Notes

## Chapter 1

1. The former polytechnics have enjoyed a less autonomous structure and ethos, but with the granting of autonomy in April 1989 (the release from LEA control) they are gaining in academic freedom while the system of higher education as a whole is becoming more fluid and diverse. This book was being written at the time of these changes and uses the term 'university' to refer to the traditional institutions, rather than to the former polytechnics.
2. Britain has a long history as a culturally diverse society and black people have long been a part of it (Fryer 1984). In recent times, the children of migrants from Britain's former colonies entering schools in the 1960s were the catalyst for a process of educational change which has been far-reaching in several respects. It reached some white rural schools as well as many multicultural urban ones and increasingly influenced all aspects of educational provision, including the school's organizational structures, ethos, curriculum and resources, and staff development programmes. To a lesser extent, post-school educational provision was also affected, with some influence, via committed individuals, reaching into the universities. This change process could be seen as a broadening and deepening educational response to ethnic diversity. Over three decades, a widening perspective influenced developments, moving the response from one of *assimilating* immigrants into 'our' society, to one of *pluralism*, giving equality of standing to all cultural groups and, finally, one of *antiracism*, concerned to counter racism in and through education.

   Such shared understandings were influenced by the work of black writers throughout the 1970s. Bernard Coard (1981), for example, showed that black children are deskilled by the schools.

## Chapter 4

1. Section 11 of the 1966 Local Government Act enables local education authorities (LEAs) to seek grant aid to meet up to three-quarters of the salary costs of teachers and others employed to meet the educational needs of students of

'New Commonwealth' or Pakistani origin, where these are 'different from or additional to' the needs of the indigenous population.

2. The 'reforms' of the 1986 and 1988 Education Reform Acts have moved in an inegaletarian direction. Though much of the Acts relates to schools (with considerable changes in local management, financial matters and curriculum, which will increase the likelihood of greater inequality between schools: Leicester 1989b), all adult education is indirectly effected by worsening school provision. Those who benefit most from schooling are also most likely to return (Woodley *et al.* 1987). Increased inequality for minority ethnic groups in schools will tend to decrease their participation in adult education and reinforce existing disproportions.

More directly, Sections 26–119 of the 1988 Act, concerning the use of school premises, will have an impact on the one million students currently enrolled in classes which meet in them, with some schools cutting non-school use and others increasing their charges.

The governing bodies of colleges of further education have increased powers. There are considerable changes in financial arrangements for colleges, which will lead to greater competitiveness and which are problematic for low-fee and part-time courses. The Act has also destabilized many existing mechanisms for offering learners access and progression through coherent local educational links, in that colleges and adult institutions will work increasingly independently of one another and of the LEA. The new 'efficiency indicators' may work against outreach programmes and non-formal community-based education, since outcomes are inevitably hard to quantify.

However, there are some (perhaps unwitting) loopholes for antiracist initiatives. With provision being more directly in the hands of each institution, this could lead to more consultation with local communities and greater flexibility and responsiveness to local interests and needs. Similarly, the great upsurge in school and college governor training associated with the Act provides an opportunity for adult educators to offer antiracist/equal opportunities education for governors.

> Creative antiracist responses to the Act ultimately fall into two categories – opportunistic and obstructive. It is possible to try to exploit the opportunities that ERA, largely unintentionally, presents through its erosion of the power of the local state (e.g. the chance to obtain more black governors). At the same time potentially racist developments such as the squeeze on part time or low/no fee courses can be opposed. The responses will sometimes come from individuals who are in a position to influence developments but also, and crucially, from groups who build, or are in, alliances of various kinds.
>
> (Leicester and Field 1990)

3. The department has had a black academic colleague who was seconded from Caribbean Studies to Continuing Education for one academic year. The department has also employed a black research assistant and departmental secretary.

# Chapter 5

1. At the time of writing, a second UCACE working group, on 'Work to Counter Education Disadvantage', was considering how best to ensure greater UCACE attention to equal opportunities issues. This group grew in part out of the earlier one and contained several of the same individuals. Two very recent positive developments have occurred. First, UFC funding has now been provided to further develop the recommendations of the first working group on Minority Ethnic Group Provision. Second, the UCACE working group on Countering Disadvantage recommended to the UCACE Council at its most recent meeting at the annual conference in April 1992 in Manchester, that UCACE establish a UCACE Standing Committee in this field. Council agreed. Richard Taylor and myself are co-chairs of this new UCACE Standing Committee.

# Chapter 6

1. Duke (1992) does not refer to Kuhn's distinction between two senses of 'paradigm', which is perhaps partly why it is not always clear whether the paradigm to which he refers is a matter of *disciplinary matrix* (shared understanding) or *achieved results* in higher education, or both, and whether or not it is already established.

# Chapter 7

1. Unfortunately, despite its Open Access policy, the Open University has not proved that it caters very well for socially disadvantaged groups. Its courses draw on high levels of literacy, rather than on the kind of life experience that can produce knowledge through reflection stimulated by discussion-based pedagogical approaches.

# Chapter 9

1. Partisan interests can influence what knowledge is pursued, and thus select *out* significant epistemological possibilities. Neglecting some dimensions of human experience (e.g. women's experience; black experience) also produces epistemological partiality.
2. The fluidity and diversity of a post-binary system of higher education with wider access, more part-time degrees and more mature students, will encourage a more diverse participation and should be seen as encouraging and requiring a more pluralist intellectual endeavour consonant with the organizational shifts.
3. Even this is a metaphorical way of talking about particular states of persons (see Rorty 1980).

4. This connection between the teaching/learning process in Higher Education and objective knowledge is a particularly close one for the field of knowledge called continuing education, whose subject matter is itself the teaching/learning process and whose aim is the improvement of teaching/learning practice. Thus the proposal made in 1988 by the Advisory Board for the Research Councils that HE institutions should be classified and funded as research, part research or teaching is potentially damaging for CE research and teaching, and is underpinned by a positivist model of research. Since teaching and research are intimately connected, conditions for good CE research are best provided by institutions which give equal emphasis to both.

5. All HE teachers should have some understanding of the learning process in relation to the second-order skills of their own discipline and some reflective practice in a variety of teaching techniques. They should also learn to distinguish the coherent structuring of experience in the meaning perspectives of their students from misunderstanding and muddle. This requires an openness to new perspectives – the ability to recognize, as valid, forms of knowledge and understanding different from their own. One is reminded of the wisdom of the old adage that the good teacher learns as much as his or her students.

6. There has been a second *philosophical* debate (Walkling 1980; Zec 1980; Phillips-Bell 1981) about selecting elements from the various cultural traditions in order to incorporate them into the curriculum. Are there overarching principles of rationality which enable us to make curriculum choices and to recognize worthwhile knowledge in other cultures, or are such principles culture-bound? I would argue that such principles (and therefore knowledge too) are not based on a-historical given foundations and thus not necessarily universally accepted. Such post-modernist anti-foundationalism has recently been seen as relevant to adult education (Westwood 1991). This present work could be seen as one in-depth exemplification of this claim.

# Bibliography

Allport, W.H. (1958) *Prejudice*. New York, Doubleday.

Apple, M. (1980) *Ideology and Curriculum*. London, Routledge.

Apple, M. (1982) *Cultural and Economic Reproduction in Education*. London, Routledge and Kegan Paul.

Bailey, R. (1984) *Beyond the Present and the Particular: A Theory of Liberal Education*. London, Routledge.

Ball, B. (1987) 'Local education policy making on equal opportunities: Corporate provision, co-option and consultation'. *Policy and Politics*, 15(2).

Barnett, R. (1990) *The Idea of Higher Education*. Milton Keynes, Society for Research into Higher Education and Open University Press.

Becher, T. and Kogan, M. (1992) *Process and Structure in Higher Education*. London, Routledge.

Ben Tovin, G. *et al.* (1986) *The Local Politics of Race*. London, Macmillan.

Brar, H.S. (1992) 'Unasked questions, impossible answers: The ethical problems of researching race and education'. In M. Leicester and M. Taylor (eds), *Ethics, Ethnicity and Education*. London, Kogan Page.

Breinburg, P. (1987) 'The black perspective in higher education'. *Multicultural Teaching*, 6(1).

Brennan, J. (1989) 'Access courses'. In O. Fulton (ed.), *Access and Institutional Change*. Milton Keynes, Society for Research into Higher Education and Open University Press.

Bright, B. (ed.) (1989) *Theory and Practice of the Study of Adult Education: The Epistemological Debate*. London, Routledge.

Brookfield, S.D. (1986) *Understanding and Facilitating Adult Learning*. New York, Oxford University Press.

Cambridge Islamic Academy (1986) *Swann Committee Report: An Evaluation from the Muslim Point of View*. Cambridge, Cambridge Islamic Academy.

Carrington, B. and Short, G. (1992) 'Researching "race" in the "all-white" primary school: the ethics of curriculum development'. In M. Leicester and M. Taylor (eds), *Ethics, Ethnicity and Education*. London, Kogan Page.

Cassera, B. (ed.) (1990) *Adult Education in a Multicultural Society*. London, Routledge.

Coard, B. (1981) 'What the British school system does to the black child'. In A. Jones and R. Jeffcoate (eds), *The School and the Multicultural Society*. London, Harper and Row.

Cole, M. (ed.) (1989) *The Social Contexts of Schooling*. Lewes, Falmer Press.

Committee of Inquiry into the Education of Children from Ethnic Minority Groups (1985) *Education for All* (the Swann Report), Cmnd 9453. London, HMSO.

Committee of Vice-Chancellors and Principals (1991) *Equal Opportunities in Employment in Universities*. London, CVCP.

Department of Education and Science (1984) *Race Relations in Schools: A Summary of Discussions at Meetings in Five Local Education Authorities*. London, DES.

Department of Education and Science (1989) *Ethnically-based Statistics on School Pupils*, Circular 16/89. London, DES.

Duke, C. (1988) 'The future shape of continuing education and universities: An inaugural lecture'. Papers in Continuing Education, No. 1. University of Warwick.

Duke, C. (1989) 'Creating the accessible institution'. In O. Fulton (ed.), *Access and Institutional Change*. Milton Keynes, Society for Research into Higher Education and Open University Press.

Duke, C. (1992) *The Learning University*. Buckingham, Open University Press.

Edgington, J. (1981) 'Is there a funding blackout?', *Voluntary Action*, Summer (2): 1.

Eggleston, S.J. *et al.* (1986) *Education for Some*. Stoke-on-Trent, Trentham.

Flew, A. (1984) *Education, Race and Revolution*. London, Centre for Policy Studies.

Freire, P. (1970) *Pedagogy of the Oppressed*. New York, Herter and Herter.

Fryer, P. (1984) *Staying Power: The History of Black People in Britain*. London, Pluto.

Fulton, O. (ed.) (1989) *Access and Institutional Change*. Milton Keynes, Society for Research into Higher Education and Open University Press.

Gilligan, C. (1982) *In a Different Voice: Psychological Theory and Women's Development*. Cambridge, MA, Harvard University Press.

Giroux, H. (1992) *Border Crossings*. London, Routledge.

Griffin, C. (1983) *Curriculum Theory in Adult and Lifelong Education*. London, Croom Helm.

Griffin, C. (1987) *Accessing Prior Learning: Progress and Practice*. London, Learning from Experience Trust.

Grinter, R. (1985) 'Bridging the gulf'. *Multicultural Teaching*, 3(2).

Halstead, M. (1988) *Education, Justice and Cultural Diversity: An Examination of the Honeyford Affair, 1984–85*. Lewes, Falmer Press.

Hatcher, R. (1987) 'Education for racial equality under attack'. *Multicultural Teacher*, 3 (Summer).

Hirst, P.H. (1965) 'Liberal education and the nature of knowledge'. In R.D. Archanboult (ed.), *Philosophical Analysis and Education*.

Hirst, P.H. and Peters, R.S. (1970) *The Logic of Education*. London, Routledge.

Home Affairs Committee (1986) *Racial Attacks and Harassment*, HC 409. London, HMSO.

Home Office (1981) *Racial Attacks: A Report of a Home Office Study*. London, Home Office.

Home Office (1989) *The Response to Racial Attack and Harassment: Guidance for Statutory Agencies*. Report of the Inter-Departmental Racial Attacks Group. London, Home Office.

Home Office (1990) *Section 11 Ethnic Minority Grants. Grant Administration: Policy and Guidelines.* London, HMSO.

Home Office (1991) *The Response to Racial Attacks: Sustaining the Momentum.* Second Report of the Inter-Departmental Racial Attacks Group. London, Home Office.

Husbands, C. (1991) 'The extreme right: A brief European overview'. *Race and Immigration*, 247, 5–14.

Jarratt, A. (1985) *Report of the Steering Committee for Efficiency Studies in Universities.* London, CVCP.

Jones, D. (1988) *Adult Education and Cultural Development.* London, Routledge.

Katz, J. (1978) *White Awareness: A Handbook for Anti-racism Training.* Oklahoma, University of Oklahoma Press.

Kelly, P.G. and Korsmeyer, C. (1991) 'Feminist scholarship and the American academy'. In P.G. Kelly and S. Slaughter (eds), *Women's Higher Education in Comparative Perspective.* The Netherlands, Kluwer.

Kelly, P.G. and Slaughter, S. (eds) (1991) *Women's Higher Education in Comparative Perspective.* The Netherlands, Kluwer.

Knowles, M.(1970) *The Modern Practice of Adult Education: Androgogy v. Pedagogy.* Surrey, Association Press.

Kohlberg, L. (1981) *The Philosophy of Moral Development.* San Francisco, Harper and Row.

Kuhn, T.S. (1962) *The Structure of Scientific Revolutions.* Chicago, IL, University of Chicago Press.

Lee, G. and Wrench, J. (1983) *Skills Seekers: Black Youth, Apprenticeships and Disadvantage.* Leicester, National Youth Bureau.

Leicester, M. (1988) 'Racism, responsibility and education'. *Journal of Philosophy of Education*, 22(2): 201–6.

Leicester, M. (1989a) 'PSE and lifelong education'. In P. White (ed.), *Personal and Social Education: Philosophical Perspectives.* The Bedford Way Series. London, Kogan Page.

Leicester, M. (1989b) *Multicultural Education: From Theory to Practice.* Windsor, NFER-Nelson.

Leicester, M. (1992) *Values, Cultural Conflict and Education.* In M. Leicester and M. Taylor (eds), *Ethics, Ethnicity and Education.* London, Kogan Page.

Leicester, M. and Field, J. (1990) 'Post-school anti-racist education after the Act'. *New Community*, 16(3): 417–23.

Leicester, M. and Lovell, T. (1991) 'Anti-racist higher education: A survey to identify good practice'. Unpublished report, Department of Continuing Education, University of Warwick.

Leicester, M. and Lovell, T. (1992) 'Comment'. *Studies in the Education of Adults*, 24(1): 214–23.

Leicester, M. and Taylor, M. (eds) (1992) *Ethics, Ethnicity and Education.* London, Kogan Page.

Lovett, T. (1983) 'Adult education and community action'. In M. Tight (ed.), *Adult Learning and Education.* London, Croom Helm.

MacDonald, I., Bhavnani, R., Khan, L. and John, G. (1989) *Murder in the Playground: Racism and Racial Violence in Manchester Schools* (the MacDonald Report). London, Longsight Press.

Madood, T. (1992) 'On not being white in Britain: Discrimination, diversity and commonality'. In M. Leicester and M. Taylor (eds), *Ethics, Ethnicity and Education*. London, Kogan Page.

Mathias, H. *et al.* (1986) 'Continuing education in universities: An innovative perspective'. *Studies in the Education of Adults*, 18(2).

Mezirow, J. (1977) 'Perspective transformation'. *Studies in Adult Education*, 9(2).

Mezirow, J. (1983) 'A critical theory of adult learning and education'. In M. Tight (ed.), *Adult Learning and Education*. London, Croom Helm.

Mezirow, J. (ed.) (1990) *Fostering Critical Reflection in Adulthood*. San Francisco, Jossey-Bass.

Mullard, C. (1984) *Anti-racist Education: The Three O's*. London, National Association for Multiracial Education.

NAB (1988) *Action for Access: Widening Opportunities in Higher Education*. London, NAB.

National Curriculum Council (1990) *The Whole Curriculum: Curriculum Guidance 3*. York, NCC.

NIACE (1989) *Adults in Higher Education: A Policy Discussion Paper*. Leicester, NIACE.

OECD (1983) *Policies for Higher Education in the 1980s*. Paris, OECD.

Pai, Y. (1990) 'Cultural pluralism, democracy and multicultural education'. In B. Cassera (ed.), *Adult Education in a Multicultural Society*. London, Routledge.

Parekh, B. (1986) 'The concept of multicultural education". In S. Modgil *et al.* (eds), *The Interminable Debate*. Lewes, Falmer Press.

Parry, G.H. (1989) 'Marking and mediating the higher education boundary'. In O. Fulton (ed.), *Access and Institutional Change*. Milton Keynes, Society for Research into Higher Education and Open University Press.

Parry, G. and Wake, C. (eds) (1990) *Access and Alternative Futures*. London, Hodder and Stoughton.

Perry, W. (1968) *Forms of Intellectual and Ethical Development in the College Years*. New York, Holt, Rinehart and Winston.

Peters, R.S. (1966) *Ethics and Education*. London, Allen and Unwin.

Phillips-Bell, M. (1981) 'A critique of Walkling and Zec'. *Journal of Philosophy of Education*, 15(1): 97–105.

Popper, K.R. (1979) *Objective Knowledge: An Evolutionary Approach*. Oxford, Clarendon Press.

Rorty, R. (1980) *Philosophy and the Mirror of Nature*. Oxford, Basil Blackwell.

Scarman, Lord (1988) *Radcliffe Lecture*. Warwick University. May.

Scott, P. (1990) 'Post-binary access and learning'. In G. Parry and C. Wake (eds), *Access and Alternative Futures*. London, Hodder and Stoughton.

Sinnott, J.D. (1984) 'Post-formal reasoning: The realistic stage'. In M.L. Commons *et al.* (eds), *Beyond Formal Operations: Late Adolescent and Adult Cognitive Development*. New York, Praeger.

Skinner, G. (1990) 'Religion, culture and education'. In P.D. Pumfrey and G.K. Verma (eds), *Race Relations and Urban Education*. Lewes, Falmer Press.

Taylor, P. (1992) *Ethnic Minority Participation in HE*. Report, Centre for Research in Ethnic Relations, University of Warwick.

Thompson, J.B. (1981) *Critical Hermenetics: A Study in the Thought of Paul Ricoeur and Jurges Habermas*. New York, Cambridge University Press.

Tight, M. (1989) 'The ideology of higher education'. In O. Fulton (ed.), *Access and Institutional Change*. Milton Keynes, Society for Research into Higher Education and Open University Press.

Todd, R. (1991) *Education in a Multicultural Society*. London, Cassell.

Troyna, B. (1987) 'Beyond multiculturalism: Towards the enactment of antiracist education in policy, provision and pedagogy'. *Oxford Review of Education*, 13(3): 307–20.

Tuckett, A. (1990) 'A higher education system fit for adult learners'. In G.H. Parry and C. Wake (eds), *Access and Alternative Futures*. London, Hodder and Stoughton.

University Council for Adult and Continuing Education (1990) *Report of the Working Party on Continuing Education Provision for the Minority Ethnic Communities*. Occasional Paper No. 2. Warwick, UCACE.

Usher, R. (1989) 'Qualification paradigms and experimental learning in higher education'. In O. Fulton (ed.), *Access and Institutional Change*. Milton Keynes, Society for Research into Higher Education and Open University Press.

Usher, R. and Bryant, B. (1989) *Adult Education as Theory, Practice and Research: The Captive Triangle*. London, Routledge.

van Dijk, T.A. (1987) *Communicating Racism: Ethnic Prejudice in Thought and Talk*. London, Sage.

van Dijk, T.A. (1991) *Racism and the Press*. London, Routledge.

Wagner, L.(1989) 'National policy and institutional development'. In O. Fulton (ed.), *Access and Institutional Change*. Milton Keynes, Society for Research into Higher Education and Open University Press.

Wain, K. (1984) 'Lifelong education: A Deweyan Challenge'. *Journal of Philosophy of Education*, 18(2).

Walkling, P. (1980) 'The idea of a multicultural curriculum'. *Journal of Philosophy of Education*, 14(1): 87–97.

Westwood, S. (1991) 'Constructing the future: A post-modern agenda for adult education'. In S. Westwood and J.E. Thomas, *The Politics of Adult Education*. Leicester, NIACE.

White, P. (ed.) (1989) *Personal and Social Education*. London, Kogan Page.

Wittgenstein, L. (1972) *Philosophical Investigations*. Oxford, Basil Blackwell.

Woodley, A. and Ellwood, S. (1989) 'Admissions, access and institutional change'. In O. Fulton (ed.), *Access and Institutional Change*. Milton Keynes, Society for Research into Higher Education and Open University Press.

Woodley, A., Wagner, L., Slowey, M. *et al.* (1987) *Choosing to Learn: Adults in Education*. Oxford University Press.

Woodrow, A. *et al.* (1987) *Choosing to Learn: Adults in Education*. Milton Keynes, Open University Press.

Young, M.F.D. (ed.) (1971) *Knowledge and Control*. London, Collier-Macmillan.

Zec, P. (1980) 'Multicultural education: What kind of relativism is possible?' *Journal of Moral Education*, 14(1): 77–87.

# Index

A levels, 61, 63
Aberystwyth University, 45
access, ix, 2, 104
    antiracist and outreach, 59–65
    CE department initiatives, 39, 43–4
    and maintaining academic
        standards, 66–76
    mature university, 51, 52, 53 57–8
access courses, 51, 53, 61, 61–3, 96
    and standards, 72–3
access movement, 59–60
accessibility, 51, 53, 60
    and antiracist university, 77–94
    boundary demolition, 64–5
    mature university, 57–8
accreditation of prior experiential
    learning (APEL), 51, 53, 61,
        63–4
accreditation of prior learning (APL),
    63–4
achieved results, 51–2
action plans, 30, 39
action research, 34–5, 36, 78–9, 84–5,
    96, 98–9
admission criteria/procedures, 43, 51,
    53, 54, 73
    access movement 60–1, 63–4
AFFOR, 36
African Caribbean Community
    Development Unit, 108
African-Caribbeans, 17–18; see also
    black people; black students;
    minority ethnic groups

Allport, W.H., 18
analytical skills, 67–8, 69, 71–2, 73
androgogy, 86–8
antiracism, viii, 21, 105, 127
    access, 59–65
    change potential, 4, 14
antiracist continuing education, 103
    conceptual clarification, 23–8
antiracist curriculum, 29–30, 89–91,
    92, 96, 130
antiracist education, 21
    characteristics, 92–3
    HE questionnaire, 95–102, 105,
        121–6
    issues, 2
    lifelong learning, 53
    mature university, 57–8
    and multicultural education, 21–2,
        92–3, 102–3
    reasons to promote, 9–10
    resources to support, 108–18
antiracist university
    curriculum, 89–91
    organization, 91–4
    research, 77–85
    teaching, 85–9
    see also mature university
Apple, M.W., 78
appointments, see staff recruitment
appraisal, staff, 56–7
Asians, 17–18; see also black people;
    black students; minority ethnic
    groups

assimilation, 127
attendance, 86–7
attitudinal changes, 87–8
awareness-raising, 21, 32, 42, 96

Bailey, R., 26
Ball, B., 13
Ball, W., 108
Barnett, R., 49–50, 50–1
Becher, T., 91–4
Ben Tovin, G., 13
Birkbeck College, 33
Birmingham Asian Resource Centre, 36
Birmingham University, 34
black organizations, 34–5, 36
black people, 17
  exploitation of researchers, 84
  professional training, 34
  *see also* African-Caribbeans; Asians; minority ethnic groups
black students
  recruitment, 40–1, 57
  targeted access courses, 62
Borthwick, A., 112
Brandt, G., 115
Brar, H.S., 84
Breinburg, P., ix
Brennan, J., 59
Bright, B., 79
Brookfield, S.D., 24
Brunel University, 99
Bryant, B., 78

Cambridge Islamic Academy, 82
Cambridge University, 42
care, ethic of, 81, 82
Carrington, B., 84
Cassara, B.B., 110
certificated courses, 33–4
citizenship, education for, 21
Coard, B., 29, 127
collaborative initiatives
  inreach, 43–4
  outreach, 28, 34–5, 45, 99
Commission for Racial Equality (CRE), 10

Committee of Vice-Chancellors and Principals (CVCP), 44–5, 60, 115–16
  academic audit-unit (AAU), 66
community
  outreach work, 28, 34–5, 45, 98–9
  pressures for change, 13
community centres, 35
competences, 74
'conscientization', 27–8, 87
consultation, 13
continuing education (CE), 4, 23, 130
  for adult educators, 32
  antiracist, *see* antiracist continuing education as change agent, 9–15
  resources to support antiracist work, 110–12
  university provision, 32–5
continuing education (CE) departments, viii
  agents for change, 2, 11–12, 51, 104, 105
  antiracism, 29–30, 103–4
  inreach and outreach, 10–12, 41–5, 104
  departmental change, *see* departmental change
  UCACE recommendations, 40–6, 103, 119–20
continuing professional and vocational education (CPVE), 34
co-option, 13
corporate action, 13
Council for National Academic Awards (CNAA), 59, 63, 66
credit accumulation and transfer (CATS), 51, 53, 63–4
critical reflection, 24–5, 27–8, 50
cultural bias, 19
cultural diversity, 14, 127; *see also* multicultural education
cultural racism, 20
cultural relativism, 103
cultural synthesis, 80, 80–1, 82–3
curriculum, 30, 61, 65
  antiracist, 29–30, 89–91, 92, 96, 130

lifelong learning, 53
paradigms of the university, 54

Dadzie, S., 108–9
decision making, 30–1, 37, 39
democratization, 30–1, 39
departmental change, 29–39
    antiracism, 29–30
    resources, 35–7
    strategies for, 30–2
    university CE provision, 32–5
    Warwick case study, 37–9
departmental ethos, 30–1, 37, 104
direct discrimination, 10
disciplinary matrix, 51–2
disciplines, academic, 68, 69–70, 71,
    79
discrimination, 28
    accredited learning movement, 64
    direct and indirect, 10
    positive, 61, 63, 97
    racial, 16, 17, 18, 19–20
    *see also* oppression; racism
distance education, 75
diversity of perspectives, 80, 81–2
Duke, C., 4, 39, 60, 66
    CE departments, 37
    paradigm shift, 51, 52, 129
    university adult education (UAE),
        11
Durham University, 41, 43
dynamic pluralism, 83

Early Years Trainers Antiracist
    Network, 112
Edgington, J., 36
Education Act (1981), 29
Education Reform Act (1988), 128
Eggleston, S.J., 96, 109
English language, 19, 29, 98
entry, *see* admission criteria/
    procedures
equal opportunities, 9, 59, 106
    CE departments, 37–8, 39, 41
    CVCP report, 44–5
    liberal and radical approaches,
        60–1

local authorities, 13
mature university, 57
social action, 28
equity, 11, 52
ethnicity, 4, 17–18, 59–60, 80–1; *see
    also* racism
experience, meaningful, 24
experiential learning
    accreditation of, 51, 53, 61, 63–4
    antiracist teaching, 88, 88–9
extramural provision, 32–4, 75

feminist perspective, 80–2
Field, J., 128
Flew, A., 21
forms of enquiry, 77–8, 79
Forum TV, 113
freedom, academic, 69
Freire, P., 87
Fryer, P., 127
Fulton, O., 60
funding, 35–7, 56–7
further education (FE), 62–3, 112–15
further education institutions, 52,
    128
Further Education Unit (FEU), 109,
    110–11, 113–15

gatekeepers, 63
Gilligan, C., 14, 74, 81–2
Giroux, H., 86
Glasgow University, 100
Goldsmiths' College, 34
good practice
    HE, 95–102, 105
    identifying, 97–102
    teaching as, 85–6
Gordon, P., 111
Gould, R., 26
governors, 128
Griffin, C., 65
Grinter, R., 90

Habermas, J., 24
Halstead, M., 20–1
Hatcher, R., 90

higher education (HE), 4, 9, 103, 104–5
antiracist university, *see* antiracist university
approaches to transformation, 105–7
collaboration with FE, 52
colleges' collaboration with universities, 43
good practice, 95–102, 105
idea of, 49–51
mass, 50, 64, 66–7, 75–6, 95
mature university, *see* mature university
pressure for change, 13–14
resources to support antiracist work, 115–16
Highlander Folk School, Tennessee, 27
Hillfields education centre, 37
Hirst, P.H., 26
history departments, 99–100
Hull University, 101

indirect discrimination, 10
inequitable outcomes, 21
injustice, 18–19, 20–1; *see also* justice
Inner London Education Authority (ILEA), 109
inreach, viii–ix
accessibility and antiracist university, 77–94
CE departments, 10–12, 41–5, 104
institutional change, 60, 61, 65, 105–7
boundary demolition and antiracist access, 64–5
liberal and radical approaches, 106–7
to mature university, 56–8
multicultural and antiracist strategies, 93
politics of, 12–13
*see also* departmental change
institutional racism, 15, 18–20, 21, 36, 102
integrational pluralism, 82
integrity, academic, 69

interdisciplinary studies, 79
interests, human, 78, 129
interviewing practice, 98
ivory tower (traditional) university paradigm, 54–5, 94

Jarratt Report, 56, 66
justice, 102, 105; *see also* injustice

Katz, J., 88, 106
Kelly, P.G., 80
Kennedy, W.B., 25
King, Martin Luther, 105–6
knowledge, 65, 72
antiracist teaching, 88, 130
diverse participation and construction of, 73, 74, 75, 80
forms of, 79–80
liberal education and, 26
perspective transformation, 24–5
power and, 78
pursuit of worthwhile, 49–51, 68
research and, 77–8, 78–9, 88
Knowles, M., 86
Kogan, M., 91–4
Kohlberg, L., 81
Korsmeyer, C., 80
Kuhn, T.S., 51–2

learning, 68
experiential, *see* experiential learning
lifelong, 23–4, 52, 53, 56, 83
*see also* pedagogy
lecturing, 70, 87; *see also* teaching
Lee, G., 19
Leicester, M., 23, 40, 56, 101
Education Reform Act, 128
institutional racism, 20
quotas, 97
Leicester University, 34–5
liberal education, 26–7, 28, 56, 92
certificated courses, 33
undermining, 50–1
*see also* perspective transformation
lifelong learning, 23–4, 52, 53, 56, 83
Liverpool University, 33, 98

local authorities, 13, 59
Local Government Act (1966), 127–8
Loughborough University, 99
Lovell, T., 40, 97, 101
Lovett, T., 35

Madood, T., 17
mainstream curriculum, 29–30
management, university, 66
management values, 91, 94
market forces university paradigm,
    54–5, 56–7, 94
market values, 91, 94
mass HE system, 50, 64, 66–7, 75–6,
    95
mathematics departments, 100–1
Mathias, H., 12
mature students
    access to HE, 63, 72–3
    CE departments, 10–11, 43–4
    mature university, 52, 53, 57
mature university, 51–6, 94
    growth into, 56–8
    see also antiracist university
meaning perspectives, 24–6, 79
    distortions in, 25–6
mental disability, 73–4
Mezirow, J., 14, 24–6, 27
minority ethnic groups
    accreditation movement, 64
    CE departments' provision, 96
    community-based work with, 34–5,
        36, 42
    students' 'special needs', 29–30,
        127–8
    targeted access courses, 62
    see also African-Caribbeans; Asians;
        black people; black students
modularization, 34, 51, 53, 64
monitoring antiracism, 99
moral development, 81–2
Mullard, C., 30
multicultural education, 83, 103, 130
    antiracist education and, 21–2,
        92–3, 102–3
    characteristics, 92–3
    HE, 89–91

'new', 90–1
    see also cultural synthesis; pluralism
*Multicultural Teaching*, 111

National Advisory Body (NAB), 57,
    59, 63
National Antiracist Movement in
    Education Team, 115
National Council for Vocational
    Qualifications (NCVQ), 62
National Curriculum, 90
Newbury, K., 110
NIACE, 85
North London Polytechnic, 61
Nottingham University, 42

open college networks (OCN), 51, 52,
    63–4
Open University, 65, 111, 129
oppression, 15
    action research and, 84–5
    social action, 27–8
    and 'voice' in HE knowledge, 73–4
    see also discrimination; racism
Organization for Economic
    Cooperation and Development
    (OECD), 14
outcomes, 18
    inequality on, 21
outreach, viii, 51, 53
    antiracist access to HE, 59–65
    CE departments, 10–12, 45, 104
Oxford University, 99

Pai, Y., 83
paradigm shifts, 51–6
paradigms of the university, 52–6,
    94
Parekh, B., 22
Parry, G., ix, 14, 57, 59
part-time degrees, 51
part-time tutors, 33
pedagogy, 53, 92
    academic standards, 68, 70, 71
    androgogy and 86–7
    see also learning; teaching
permeation, 45

perspective transformation, 23–6, 79
Peters, R.S., 26, 68
Phillips-Bell, M., 130
pluralism, 14, 20, 92, 105, 127, 129
  competing perspectives, 82–3
  *see also* multicultural education
policy statements, 31, 96
polytechnics, former, 127
Polytechnics Central Admissions
    System (PCAS), 59–60
'pool of talent', 66–7
positive action, 44–5, 97
positive discrimination, 61, 63, 97
post-modernist research model, 78–9
power
  antiracist teaching, 88
  knowledge and, 78
  race-related research, 84
  racism, 16–17, 19–20
prejudice, 16–17, 17–18, 89, 102; *see
    also* discrimination; racism
professional training, 34
professional values, 91, 94
publicity, 98

quality, 66–9, 105; *see also* standards
questionnaire, HE antiracist, 95–102,
    105, 121–6
quotas, 97

race, as cutting edge, 14–15
race-related research, 84–5
Race Relations Act (1976), 9–10, 18,
    34, 44
racism, 16–21, 87–8, 89, 102
  awareness courses, 32
  lifelong learning, 53
  perspective transformation and,
    25–6
  *see also* antiracism
rationality/reasoning, 26, 50
realism, 78–9
reflection, critical, 24–5, 27–8, 50
research, 51, 70, 88, 130
  antiracist, 77–85
  CE departments and participatory,
    34–5

enriching, 81–3, 104–5
feminist perspective, 80–2
forms of knowledge, 79–80
paradigms of the university, 54
post-modernist model, 78–9
race-related, 84–5
revolutionary and normal, 77–8
resistance to change, 19
resources
  antiracist work, 108–18
  funding, 35–7, 56–7
revolutionary research, 77–8
Rorty, R., 129
Runnymede Trust, 110

Sammons, P., 110
schools, 33, 127, 128
  separate, 82
Scott, P., 66–7
second-chance-to-learn courses, 63–4
Sex Discrimination Act (1975), 44
Short, G., 84
short-term funding, 35
Shukla, K., 115
skills, academic, 67–8, 69, 71–2, 73
social action, 11, 27–8, 34–5, 36, 92
social utility, 94
Southampton University, 41, 42, 45
'special needs', 29, 127–8
staff appraisal, 56–7
staff development, 39, 41, 42–3, 96,
    101
staff recruitment, 32, 39, 41, 96, 97,
    101
  good practice, 97–8
  Warwick University CE department,
    38
standards, academic, 54, 66–76
  educational change and
    maintaining, 72–6
  interrelated aspects, 69–72
  quality debate, 66–9
stereotypes, 17–18
structural racism, 20
student loans, 36–7
student recruitment, 40–1, 57, 96
support staff, 39

Swann Report, 1, 18, 82
syncretism (cultural synthesis), 80,
    80-1, 82-3

targeted access courses, 62
Taylor, P., 2, 60
teaching, 51, 103, 104, 130
    academic standards, 68, 70, 71, 75
    androgogy and good, 86-8
    antiracist, 85-6, 88-9
    as good practice, 85-6
    paradigms of the university, 54
    *see also* pedagogy
Thompson, J.B., 24
Tight, M., 64
Todd, R., 20
tolerance, 82
Trade Union and Basic Education
    Project (TUBE), 111
traditional university paradigm, 54-5,
    94
Troyna, B., 90
Tuckett, A., 86

understanding, 49-50, 69; *see also*
    knowledge
Unit for the Development of Adult
    Continuing Education (UDACE),
    110
university adult education (UAE),
    11
University Central Council on
    Admissions (UCCA), 59-60
University Council for Adult and
    Continuing Education (UCACE),
    10, 62, 104
    Countering Disadvantage working
        group, 129
    Minority Ethnic Group Provision

working group, 40, 44, 45,
    119-20
University Funding Council (UFC),
    35, 52, 56
Usher, R., 64, 78

values, 3, 54, 88-9, 92
    academic virtues, 68-9, 70-1, 76
    university organization, 91-4
Van Dijk, T.A., 17
virtues, academic, 68-9, 70-1, 76
vocational education, 50
vocational qualifications, 62-3
voices, disempowered, 74

Wagner, L., 59
Wain, K., 23
Wake, C., 14, 59
Walkling, P., 130
Warwick University, 33, 72
    CE department, 37-9
    Centre for Ethnic Relations, 60
    Open Studies Programme, 37, 38
welfarism, 94
Westwood, S., 130
Williams, J., 116
women's experience, 74, 80-2
women's studies, 80
Woodley, A., 128
Woodrow, A., 64
'word-of-mouth recruitment', 19
Workers' Education Association
    (WEA), 99, 112
Wrench, J., 19

York University, 100
Young, M.F.D., 78

Zec, P., 130

# The Society for Research into Higher Education

The Society for Research into Higher Education exists to stimulate and co-ordinate research into all aspects of higher education. It aims to improve the quality of higher education through the encouragement of debate and publication on issues of policy, on the organization and management of higher education institutions, and on the curriculum and teaching methods.

The Society's income is derived from subscriptions, sales of its books and journals, conference fees and grants. It receives no subsidies, and is wholly independent. Its individual members include teachers, researchers, managers and students. Its corporate members are institutions of higher education, research institutes, professional, industrial and governmental bodies. Members are not only from the UK, but from elsewhere in Europe, from America, Canada and Australasia, and it regards its international work as amongst its most important activities.

Under the imprint *SRHE & Open University Press*, the Society is a specialist publisher of research, having some 45 titles in print. The Editorial Board of the Society's Imprint seeks authoritative research or study in the above fields. It offers competitive royalties, a highly recognizable format in both hard- and paperback and the world-wide reputation of the Open University Press.

The Society also publishes *Studies in Higher Education* (three times a year), which is mainly concerned with academic issues, *Higher Education Quarterly* (formerly *Universities Quarterly*), mainly concerned with policy issues, *Research into Higher Education Abstracts* (three times a year), and *SRHE News* (four times a year).

The Society holds a major annual conference in December, jointly with an institution of higher education. In 1990, the topic was 'Industry and Higher Education', at and with the University of Surrey. In 1991, it was 'Research and Higher Education in Europe', with the University of Leicester. Conferences have included, in 1992, 'Learning to Effect', with Nottingham Polytechnic, and in 1993, 'Governments and the Higher Education Curriculum' with the University of Sussex. In addition it holds regular seminars and consultations on topics of current interest.

The Society's committees, study groups and branches are run by the members. The groups at present include:

Teacher Education Study Group
Continuing Education Group
Staff Development Group
Excellence in Teaching and Learning
Women in Higher Education Group

# Benefits to members

## *Individual*

Individual members receive:

- *SRHE News*, the Society's publications list, conference details and other material included in mailings.
- Greatly reduced rates for *Studies in Higher Education* and *Higher Education Quarterly*.
- A 35% discount on all Open University Press & SRHE publications.
- Free copies of the Precedings – commissioned papers on the theme of the Annual Conference.
- Free copies of *Research into Higher Education Abstracts*.
- Reduced rates for conferences.
- Extensive contacts and scope for facilitating initiatives.
- Reduced reciprocal memberships.

## *Corporate*

Corporate members receive:

- All benefits of individual members, plus
- Free copies of *Studies in Higher Education.*
- Unlimited copies of the Society's publications at reduced rates.
- Special rates for its members e.g. to the Annual Conference.

**SRHE**

*Membership details:* SRHE, 344–354 Gray's Inn Road, London, WC1X 8BP, UK. Tel: 071 837 7880
*Catalogue:* SRHE & Open University Press, Celtic Court, 22 Ballmoor, Buckingham MK18 1XW. Tel: (0280) 823388

**ADULTS WITH LEARNING DIFFICULTIES**
EDUCATION FOR CHOICE AND EMPOWERMENT:
A HANDBOOK OF GOOD PRACTICE

**Jeannie Sutcliffe**

'I want to learn about Jesus and history and thunder and lightning.'

With support from the Joseph Rowntree Foundation, the National Institute of Adult Continuing Education (NIACE) set out to highlight good practice in continuing education for adults with learning difficulties. This handbook is one outcome of that project, and provides a broadly-based practical approach for staff working in a teaching or enabling role with adults who have learning difficulties.

A variety of innovative practice is described, drawn from settings where students are actively involved in choosing what and how they learn. The handbook's format encourages busy practitioners and managers to reflect on their own provision, and opportunities for development through student empowerment within a multi-agency framework are stressed.

***Contents***
*Using this handbook – Self advocacy and citizen advocacy – Learning choices – Ways and means of learning – Learning for a purpose – Integration – Students with learning difficulties and additional complications – Transition to community living – Education of the wider community – Issues for managers and planners – Glossary – Useful addresses – Index.*

200pp    0 335 09609 3 (Paperback)

# THE TEXTS OF PAULO FREIRE

Paul V. Taylor

Paulo Freire can be numbered among the few, great educators this century. His classroom is the world of the oppressed: his subject is the literacy of liberation.

This volume provides a (re)introduction to Freire. The first part is a fresh, biographical sketch of his life, the context within which he worked and the texts which he has produced. The second part uncovers the genius of his eclecticism and discovers that, contrary to the myth, his revolutionary method is more a radical reinvention of classical pedagogy.

This sets the scene for a review and questioning of Freire's method and of his philosophy of contradiction. There is then a critical examination of his view of literacy through a close reading of the teaching material on which his successful method is based.

The concluding section attempts to reconstruct a practice of literacy, illustrating the importance of Freire's pedagogy of questioning for all those who are working in the field of literacy today.

### Contents
*Introduction: the textualizing and contextualizing of Freire – A biographical sketch – Backgrounds and borrowings: a review of selected sources and influences – Education and liberation: the means and ends of Dialogue and Conscientization – The 'Método Paulo Freire': generative words and generating literacy – Generating literacy: decoding Freire's ten learning situations – A reconstruction of literacy – Conclusion – Notes – Bibliographies – Index.*

176pp    0 335 19019 7 (Paperback)    0 335 19020 0 (Hardback)

# HIGHER EDUCATION: A PART-TIME PERSPECTIVE

## Malcolm Tight

*Higher Education: A Part-time Perspective* aims to provide a comprehensive analysis of the past, present and future of part-time higher education in the United Kingdom. It examines the institutions and students involved, and describes the various kinds of provision available. The current provision in the United Kingdom is related to its historical development, and compared with the position in other developed countries.

But this is not *just* a book about part-time higher education. By looking at higher education from a part-time perspective, we can enlarge our understanding of higher education as a whole. The final part of the book attempts to do this by comparing the value of part-time and full-time forms of provision. Alternative models of higher education are explored, and the prospects for future development are reviewed. The book concludes that, while part-time higher education has been seriously under-valued in recent years, it offers the only viable model for a significantly expanded, more flexible and more relevant higher education system in the future.

### Contents
*Definition and scope – History – The current position – International comparisons – Providers and provision – Students and clients – Value and purpose – Alternative models – Prospects and conclusions – References – Index.*

192pp    0 335 09610 7 (Paperback)    0 335 09611 5 (Hardback)